MEGASTRUCTURES
TALLEST · LONGEST · BIGGEST · DEEPEST

Ian Graham

QED Publishing

Created for QED Publishing by Tall Tree Ltd
www.talltreebooks.co.uk
Editor: Rob Colson
Designers: Malcolm Parchment and
    Jonathan Vipond
Illustrations: Apple Illustration and
    Caroline Watsonw

Copyright © QED Publishing 2011

First published in the UK in 2011 by
QED Publishing
A Quarto Group company
226 City Road
London EC1V 2TT

www.qed-publishing.co.uk

A catalogue record for this book is
available from the British Library.

ISBN 978 1 84835 804 1

Printed in China

Picture credits
(t=top, b=bottom, l=left, r=right, c=centre)
44-45 David Lee Photography; 45 Lee Jackson; 46
BLS AG; 56-57 Markuskun; 62-63 Femern AS
Alamy: 8-9 Michael Doolittle/Alamy, 10 kpzfoto,
14 DBURKE, 39t Thomas Jackson; 46-47 qaphotos.
com; 47 qaphotos.com; 53 Dominic Twist; 57
David R. Frazier Photolibrary, Inc. 67b Picture
Contact BV, 89 Christine Osborne Pictures, 98t
Doug Steley, 102t Danita Delimont, 107 Tom Tracy
Photography, 110l QA Photos.com, 119l Ady Kerry;
Andy Pernick 84b; **Bill Ebbesen** 109c; **BP** 116l;
116-117; **Corbis** 13t Joel W. Rogers, 13b Joel W.
Rogers, 19 Sean Aidan, Eye Ubiquitous/CORBIS,
24-25 Jose Fuste Raga/CORBIS, 26-27 pix2go;
37b Mark Thiessen/National Geographic Society; 40
Imaginechina; 41t Frederic Stevens/epa; 62 Jacques
Langevin/Sygma; 52-53 Andrew Kendrick/US Coast
Guard; 54-55 Stringer/China/Reuters; 61 Bettmann; 62
Jacques Langevin/Sygma; 66 Xinhua Press, 66b Erich
Schlegel, 69 Bettmann, 71 David Gray/Reuters, 77,
Charles Lenars, 78 Danny Lehman, 87 Ed Kashi, 88t
Jorge Ferrari/epa, 90t Andy Clark/X00056/Reuters, 90b
Christopher Morris/VII, 93 Neil Tingle; 97b Paull A
Souders, 100-101 Staff/Reuters, 103b Peter Andrews/
Reuters, 104 Cezaro de Luca/epa, 105t Nadeem
Khawer/epa, 110l Pascal Rossignol/Reuters, 110r
Jacques Langevin/Sygma, 112-113 Najla Feanny, 112t
Tom Fox/Dallas Morning News, 115r George Steinmetz,
118l Stefan Wermuth/Reuters; **Creative Commons** 21t
Joi Ito, 24 Ratsbew, 25 Trubshaw, 29 Statoil;
Dreamstime 12 Stuart Pearcey; Getty images 11
Science & Society Picture, 15, 39b Redeyed, 115l
Natalia Bratslavsky; **Eurotunnel** 111t; **Getty Images**, 20t
Bloomberg, 20b Barcroft Media, 21b AFP; 44 Cleland
Rimmer/Fox Photos; 52b AFP; 58 Hulton Archive, 79t
William West/AFP, 91 AFP, 97t Joe Raedle, 105b Hulton
Archive, 111r AFP/Denis Charlet; **Gump Stump** 98-99;
HKS 68; **istockphoto** 6-7 Mlenny Photography;
Shutterstock 10-11 Shutterstock, 14-15 Cupertino, 16-17
WH Chow, 16 Jessmine, 17 Songquan Deng, 18 Henryk
Sadura, 20-21 Philip Lange, 22-23 Elena Yakusheva, 22
Alexander Chaikin, 26 Rorem, 30-31, 101b Eduard
Andras, 120-121 Robas; **London 2012** 80, 81; **Markus
Schweiss** 102-103; **NASA** 86; **NJR ZA** 72b; **Photolibrary**
41b Thomas Frey, 99 The Print Collector; **Populous** 92;
Risto Kaijaluoto 109; Shutterstock 96 Arnold John
Labrentz, 106-107 Lee Prince, 113t Kola-Kola, 119r
Natalia Bratslavsky; **Shutterstock**, 30 Bart J, 36-37
Jarno Gonzalez Zarraonandia; 37t Francisco
Caravana 38-39 Laitr Keiows; 42-43 Manamana; 43t
SVLuma; 43b clearviewstock; 48-49 Brendan Howard;
50-51 Antony McAulay; 51l E. Petersen; 55t Luis Santos;
58-59 Rafael Ramirez Lee; 59 Shutterstock; 60-61 r.nagy,
70 Caitlin Mirra, 72t prism68, 73 oksana.perkins, 74
Dudarev Mikhail, 75 Asier Villafranca, 75c Daniel M.
Nagy, 76 Tom Cummins, 78 Gary718, 79b Chunni4691,
83 Joop Hoek, 84t Andy Z, 87 frontpage, 85 Elzbieta
Sekowska, 88b Meewezen Photography; **US
Government** 117t; **Uploader** 85

Words in **bold** are explained in the Glossary
on page 124.

Contents

TOWERING GIANTS AND OTHER TALL MEGASTRUCTURES

Top 10 tallest skyscrapers

Skyscraper	Location	Height
Burj Khalifa	Dubai, UAE	828 m
Taipei 101	Taipei, Taiwan	508 m
Shanghai World Financial Centre	Shanghai, China	492 m
International Commerce Centre	Hong Kong, China	484 m
Petronas Towers	Kuala Lumpur, Malaysia	452 m
Greenland Financial Centre	Nanjing, China	450 m
Willis Tower	Chicago, USA	442 m
International Finance Centre	Guangzhou, China	440 m
Jin Mao Tower	Shanghai, China	421 m
Two International Finance Centre	Hong Kong, China	415 m

People have been fascinated by the construction of tall structures for thousands of years. Buildings that made everyone look skywards inspired awe and emphasized a ruler's wealth and power. Today, the tallest buildings are still expressions of wealth and power. They become famous and they make the places where they are built famous too.

Where are they built?

The tallest buildings are very expensive to construct, so they are usually built in the wealthiest parts of the world. For most of the 20th century, the world's tallest buildings were built only in North America. By the 1990s, countries such as Malaysia and Taiwan were building record-breaking skyscrapers. As China became wealthier in the 1990s and early 2000s, new skyscrapers were built in Chinese cities including Shanghai, Nanjing, Guangzhou and Shenzhen. Today, the astonishing 828-metre Burj Khalifa in Dubai is the world's tallest skyscraper.

Why are they built?

Skyscrapers are built for practical reasons as well as for fame. Land in big cities is very expensive. By building upwards instead of spreading out across the ground, skyscrapers have a small **footprint**, but they pack a lot of homes, hotel rooms and offices into this small area. The tallest towers are useful in other ways too. They send radio and television signals over hills and tall buildings.

MEGA FACTS

The world's first skyscraper was the Home Insurance Building in Chicago, USA. It was built in 1885 and was 10 storeys high. It was demolished in 1931.

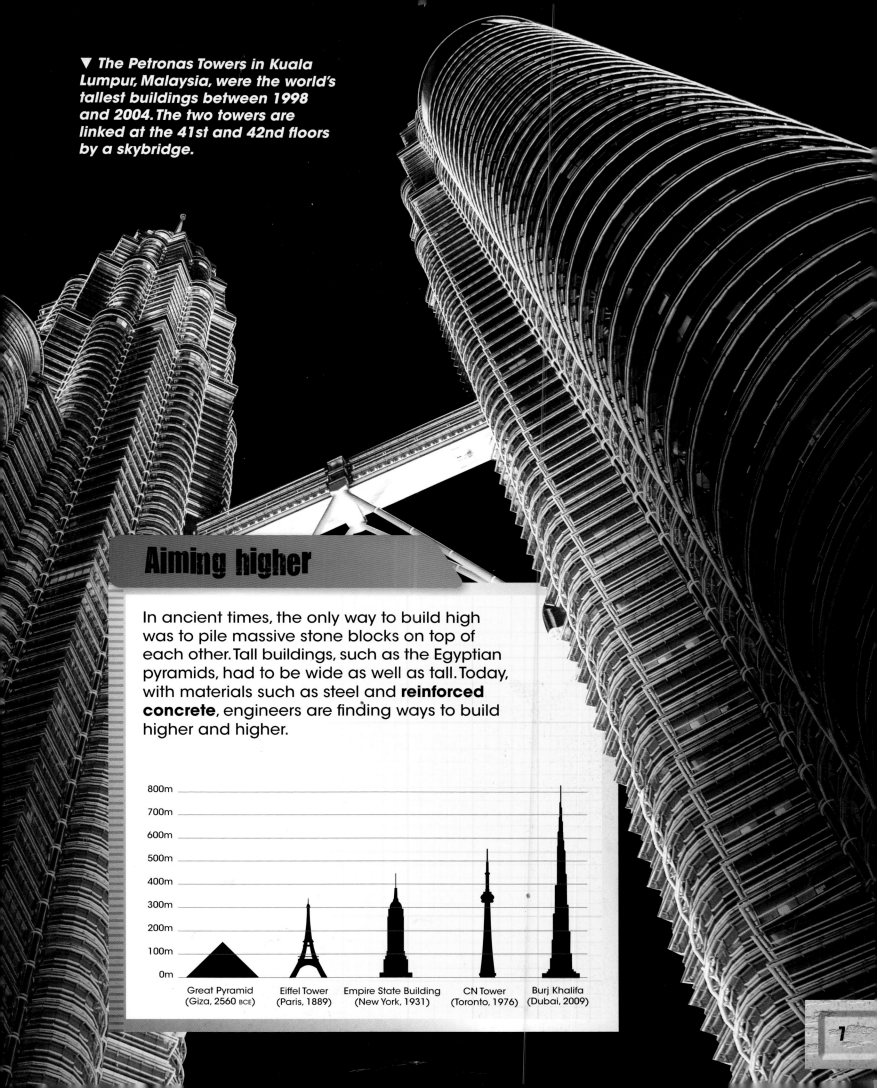

▼ *The Petronas Towers in Kuala Lumpur, Malaysia, were the world's tallest buildings between 1998 and 2004. The two towers are linked at the 41st and 42nd floors by a skybridge.*

Aiming higher

In ancient times, the only way to build high was to pile massive stone blocks on top of each other. Tall buildings, such as the Egyptian pyramids, had to be wide as well as tall. Today, with materials such as steel and **reinforced concrete**, engineers are finding ways to build higher and higher.

800m				
700m				
600m				
500m				
400m				
300m				
200m				
100m				
0m				
Great Pyramid (Giza, 2560 BCE)	Eiffel Tower (Paris, 1889)	Empire State Building (New York, 1931)	CN Tower (Toronto, 1976)	Burj Khalifa (Dubai, 2009)

Superstructures

The part of a skyscraper or tower that is above the ground, called the **superstructure**, is supported by another part hidden under the ground, called the **substructure**. The substructure stops the building from sinking into the ground, and also helps to prevent the whole structure from falling over.

Supporting the weight

The weight of a house is held up by its walls. They are called **load-bearing walls**. If a skyscraper had load-bearing walls, they would have to be so thick that they would fill the base of the building. Instead, a skyscraper is held up by a frame that is usually made of steel. Thin walls, called **curtain walls**, hang from the building's frame like curtains.

The first skyscrapers

The 16-storey Monadnock Building in Chicago, USA, was one of the world's first skyscrapers. The northern half of the building was built using load-bearing walls, which are nearly 2 metres thick at the base. The southern half of the building was built using a steel frame and curtain walls like a modern skyscraper. The thin curtain walls create more space inside, especially on the ground floor.

▶ Inside a skyscraper there is a strong frame. It supports the building's weight so that the walls can be very thin.

Underground legs

A skyscraper or tower stands on a small base, like a pencil standing on end. A pencil falls over very easily, but skyscrapers and towers must not topple. To stop this happening, they are anchored to **concrete** and steel legs, called **piles**, that extend deep underground. The piles rest on solid rock or a concrete platform. This supports the building's weight and stops it from sinking. The piles also work like a tree's roots to hold the building upright. If the building tries to lean over, the ground grips the piles and holds it steady.

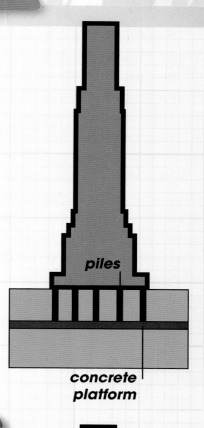

piles

concrete platform

▶ Piles sit on the hard rock beneath the soil or on a specially constructed concrete platform.

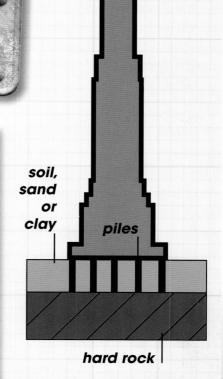

soil, sand or clay

piles

hard rock

MEGA FACTS

The Willis Tower in Chicago was the world's tallest skyscraper when it was completed in 1974. It is 442 metres high and weighs 222,500 tonnes.

Standing up to nature

Once a skyscraper is built, it has to withstand everything that nature throws at it. It might face hurricane-strength winds or shaking caused by an earthquake. Engineers use models, test rigs and computer programs to ensure that wind and shaking will not cause problems.

The big blow

To withstand the pressure, or pushing force, of the wind, today's super-tall skyscrapers have to be 50 times stronger than a 60-metre building of the 1940s. Model skyscrapers are placed in wind tunnels to study how the wind blows around them and to measure the wind pressure on the walls and windows. Computer models are used to show how the building bends and shakes, and to spot any weaknesses in the structure.

Wind tunnel testing

This model of a skyscraper and the buildings around it was built to be placed in a wind tunnel for testing. The model is on a turntable, which can be rotated to study the effects of wind blowing from different directions.

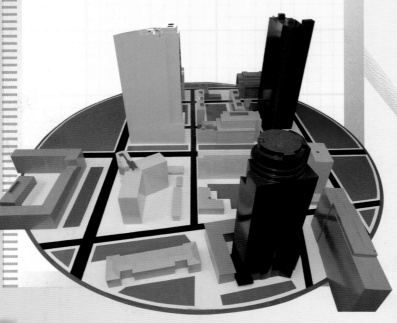

▼ This massive ball is the 660-tonne tuned mass damper in Taipei 101, a skyscraper in Taiwan.

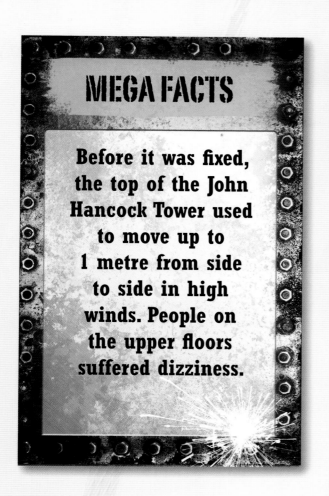

Shakin' all over

When the John Hancock Tower was built in Boston, USA, in the 1970s, it swayed and twisted in the wind much more than expected. The swaying and twisting motions were happening in time with each other. This is called **resonance**, and it can make a building shake dangerously. One way to protect a building from resonance is to use a **tuned mass damper**. This is a heavy chunk of metal that can move from side to side. When the building sways in one direction, the damper moves in the opposite direction, tugging the building back and stopping it from swaying too much. Tuned mass dampers and 1360 tonnes of steel beams, called braces, cured the John Hancock Tower's swaying.

▶ **Taipei 101's tuned mass damper hangs from the building's 92nd floor down to the 88th floor.**

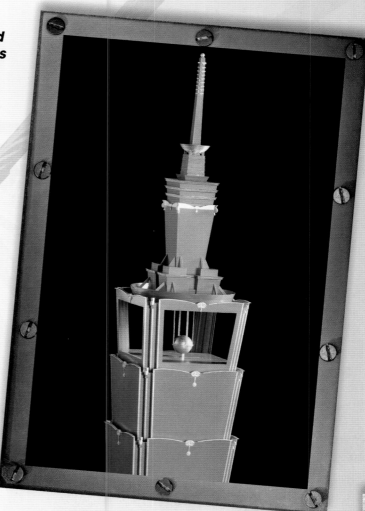

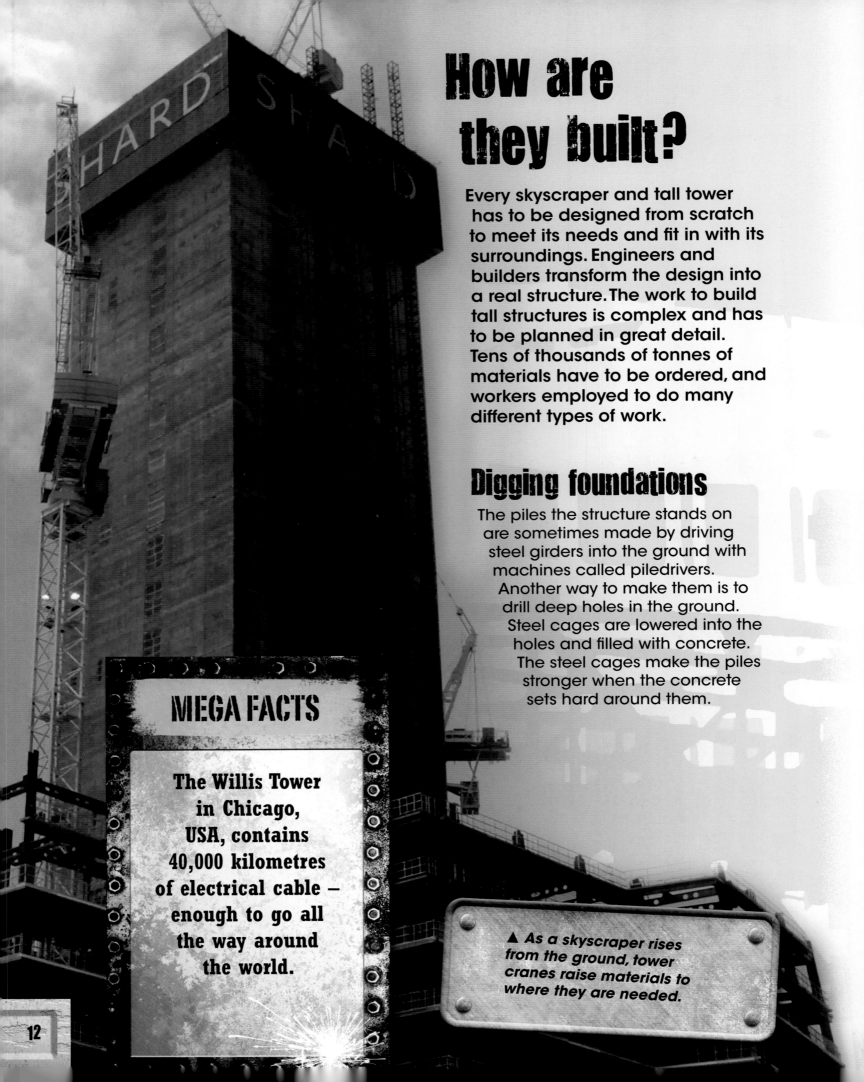

How are they built?

Every skyscraper and tall tower has to be designed from scratch to meet its needs and fit in with its surroundings. Engineers and builders transform the design into a real structure. The work to build tall structures is complex and has to be planned in great detail. Tens of thousands of tonnes of materials have to be ordered, and workers employed to do many different types of work.

Digging foundations

The piles the structure stands on are sometimes made by driving steel girders into the ground with machines called piledrivers. Another way to make them is to drill deep holes in the ground. Steel cages are lowered into the holes and filled with concrete. The steel cages make the piles stronger when the concrete sets hard around them.

MEGA FACTS

The Willis Tower in Chicago, USA, contains 40,000 kilometres of electrical cable – enough to go all the way around the world.

▲ As a skyscraper rises from the ground, tower cranes raise materials to where they are needed.

Floors and walls

The floors are made by laying steel panels, called **decking**, between the beams. Concrete is poured on the decking to make the floors. The exterior wall panels are attached to the outside of the building's frame. A crane lifts them into position and workers bolt them in place.

▶ *Workers have laid out decking to make a floor in this skyscraper. Now they are pouring concrete on top and levelling it.*

Framing up

The building's steel frame is built on top of the piles. The frames of older buildings, such as the Empire State Building in New York City, USA, were held together using iron pins called **rivets**. Since the 1950s, skyscraper frames have been bolted or **welded** together.

Finishing touches

Once the frame has been completed, there is still a vast amount of work to be done. The electrical cabling, lighting, plumbing and air conditioning have to be installed. The interior walls and ceilings have to be fitted too.

▼ *A welder welds parts of a skyscraper's steel frame together. He wears a visor to protect his eyes from the bright flames.*

Finishing touches

The building's steel frame was finished in September 2007 and the **cladding** was completed by June 2008. The Shanghai World Financial Centre opened on 28 August 2008.

▲ The cladding panels were lifted into position by two tower cranes.

In the 1990s, a new skyscraper was planned for Shanghai, China. The Shanghai World Financial Centre was to be 460 metres high, making it the world's tallest building.

Construction began in 1997, but stopped due to a shortage of money. It started again six years later. The delay meant that by the time the building was finished, Taipei 101 in Taiwan had become the world's tallest building at 508 metres high. Plans were made to change the design of the Shanghai skyscraper so that it would be higher than Taipei 101, but the tallest it could go was 492 metres.

Shanghai World Financial Centre

height: 492 metres

▼ The original design for the Shanghai World Financial Centre was a tall, graceful, tapering tower with a circular hole at the top.

Changing shape

The hole near the top was originally designed to be round, but this was thought to look too much like the Japanese flag, so it was changed to an angular shape.

▶ The Shanghai World Financial Centre has 101 floors above ground and three floors below ground.

MEGA FACTS

If there is a fire in the building, people can go to one of its fireproof floors, called refuge floors, where they can wait to be rescued.

location: Shanghai, China

Famous giants

There are thousands of skyscrapers, towers and other tall structures all over the world. Some of them are so distinctive that they are instantly recognizable. The Great Pyramid, the Leaning Tower of Pisa and the Empire State Building are among the world's most famous tall structures. Between them, they span 4500 years of history.

The Great Pyramid

Built at Giza in Egypt in about 2560 BCE as a tomb for Pharaoh Khufu, the Great Pyramid was the world's tallest artificial structure for 4000 years. It stands 146 metres high and the base is 230 metres long on each side. It was built from 2.3 million stone blocks weighing up to 13.6 tonnes each. It was originally clad in white limestone, but this was later stripped away and used to build other tombs or temples.

The Leaning Tower of Pisa

This famous leaning tower was built in Pisa, Italy, in the 12th century. It started sinking on one side, and leaning over, when it was only three floors high. Over the centuries, there were several attempts to stop it leaning further, but they all failed. Then in 1998, soil was removed from beneath the non-sinking side of the tower. This straightened up the tower a little and saved it from collapsing.

▼ At the top, the Leaning Tower of Pisa leans nearly 4 metres from the vertical.

▼ The observation deck is located on the 124th floor, about two-thirds of the way up. Two high-speed lifts carry visitors up to the deck in just three minutes.

Glass cladding

The superstructure is covered with a metal and glass cladding. Its 24,830 glass panels had to be cut to size by hand. The cladding has to be able to stand up to the extreme daytime heat and cooler nights of Dubai.

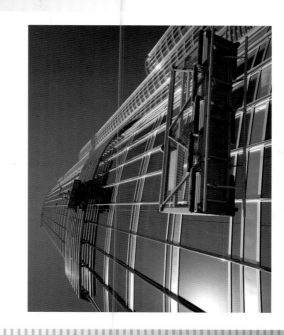

▲ As it neared completion, the finishing touches were made to the cladding by workers in special moving platforms called gondolas.

▼ *The Great Pyramid of Giza is the only one of the Seven Wonders of the Ancient World still standing.*

The Empire State Building was built in New York City, USA, in 1931. It was the first building to use the fast-track construction method that is commonly used today. To save time and cut costs, construction work began while the building was still being designed. It was built around a strong central core containing the lift shafts. The outside of the building is covered with limestone and stainless steel. It was built in just 410 days, and at 381 metres high excluding the spire, it was the tallest building in the world for 41 years.

▶ *The Empire State Building was designed with an airship terminal at the top. The plan was for passenger airships to tie up to the 62-metre spire. However, strong winds blowing up the side of the building made it too dangerous so the terminal was cancelled.*

spire

MEGA FACTS

From 1930 to 1931, three skyscrapers were built in New York City: first came 40 Wall Street, then the Chrysler Building, and finally the Empire State Building.

Skyscrapers

The first skyscrapers were built in the 1880s in Chicago, USA. They were about 10 floors high, but skyscrapers have been getting taller and taller ever since. The height of modern skyscrapers and towers presents many engineering problems. Imagine having to take the stairs to your apartment or office on the 60th floor every day! The skyscrapers and towers that have shaped modern cities might never have been built if the lift had not been invented. Cleaning windows hundreds of metres above the ground presents another major problem.

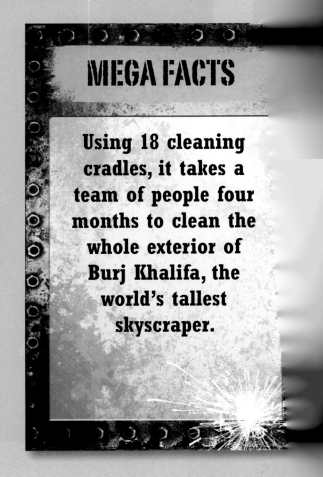

MEGA FACTS

Using 18 cleaning cradles, it takes a team of people four months to clean the whole exterior of Burj Khalifa, the world's tallest skyscraper.

Cleaning windows

Skyscrapers are covered with thousands of windows and all of them have to be cleaned. Window cleaners often work in cradles hanging down from a skyscraper's roof. The cleaner can move the cradle up, down and sideways, to reach all the windows. Today, robot window cleaners are beginning to take over some of this work.

◀ *Skyscraper window cleaners need a good head for heights as they hang down outside the building, sometimes hundreds of metres above the ground.*

Burj Khalifa

height: 828 metres

**The shimmering silver skyscraper Burj Khalifa in Dubai is by far the world's tallest building. It is so tall that it casts a shadow on clouds that glide below its glistening steel spire.
It contains homes for 25,000 people, plus a hotel, shops and offices. Work on the building's superstructure began in March 2005 and was completed in 2009.**

Unlike most skyscrapers, Burj Khalifa has a concrete internal structure instead of a steel frame. A steel frame would have made the building too expensive. It would also have made the tall, slender building too flexible – it would have swayed too much in the wind.

Burj Khalifa's Y-shaped design is called a buttressed core. The shape of the core provides torsional stability, which means that it resists twisting forces caused by the wind. The wings buttress (support) the core and each other.

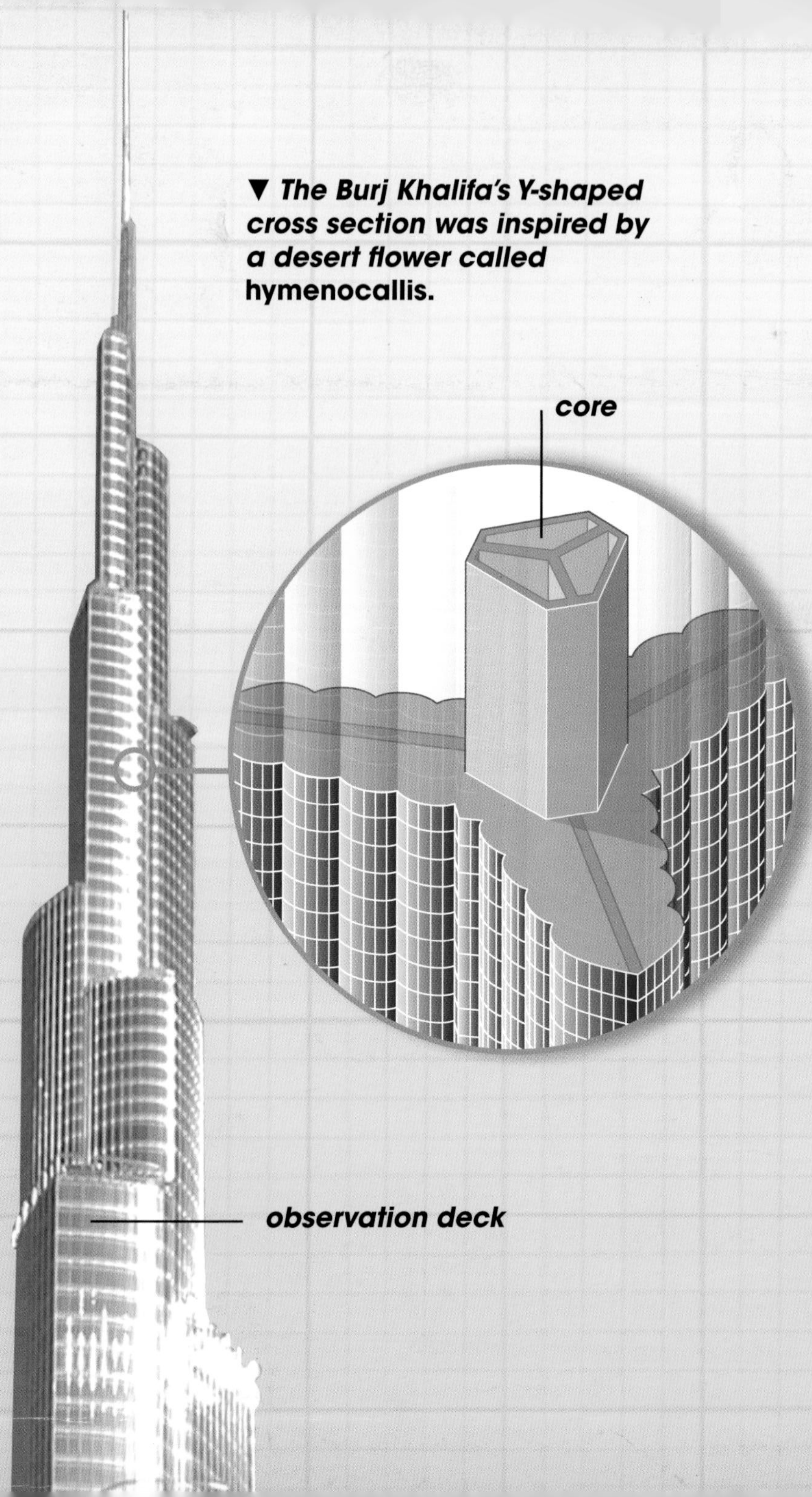
core
observation deck

▼ ***The Burj Khalifa's Y-shaped cross section was inspired by a desert flower called*** **hymenocallis.**

Going up

The first public passenger lift was installed in Haughwout's Department Store in New York City, USA, in 1857. As skyscrapers become taller and taller, their lifts have to move faster and faster to stop journeys up and down the building taking too long. The fastest skyscraper lifts travel at more than 60 kilometres per hour.

Heating and cooling

A skyscraper's windows do not open to let in fresh air, so air has to be pumped through the building. The air is heated or cooled to maintain a comfortable temperature. A lot of equipment is needed to supply the air and also the water and waste removal services. For about every 10 floors of offices or apartments, a whole floor is set aside for equipment. These are called mechanical floors.

◄ The lifts on the Lloyd's Building in London, UK, run up and down outside the building.

▲ The lower floors up to level eight are taken up by a luxury hotel designed by the Italian fashion designer Giorgio Armani.

MEGA FACTS

Residents and workers can make their way up and down Burj Khalifa by means of 57 lifts, eight escalators and 2909 stairs.

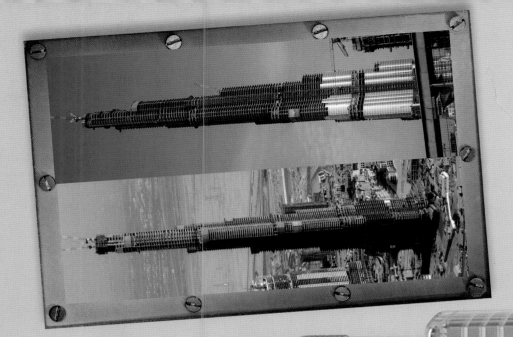

▼ The concrete structure was built first. It is strengthened with 31,400 tonnes of steel bars (left). After it was completed, the glass and steel cladding were fitted around the concrete (right).

Water supplies

A giant building needs an enormous amount of water for its occupants. Burj Khalifa's water system distributes 946,000 litres of water through the building each day. It comes from desalination plants that convert salty seawater into fresh drinking water.

Air conditioning

The tower is so tall that the temperature outside it is 7 degrees Celsius lower at the top than at the base. This air is sucked into the building to help cool it, using a technique called 'skysourcing'.

▲ By the time the cladding was added to the outside, Burj Khalifa was taller than two Empire State Buildings stacked on top of each other.

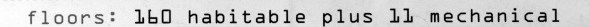

floors: 160 habitable plus 11 mechanical

The Eiffel Tower was built as a monument to the French Revolution. It was completed in 1889. At a height of 312 metres, it was the world's tallest man-made structure. Today, communications **antennae** have raised its height to 324 metres. It was constructed from 18,038 pieces of iron. Its designer, Gustave Eiffel, was one of the first people to realize the importance of wind forces on tall structures. He designed the tower as an open lattice through which the wind could blow.

▶ The Eiffel Tower's iron structure is protected from rusting by paint. It is repainted every seven years. The job takes 25 painters more than a year and needs 60 tonnes of paint.

Mighty monuments

Monuments are structures built to remember people or events. They may be statues, columns, tombs, temples or other permanent structures. Two of the most instantly recognizable monuments are the Statue of Liberty in New York City, USA, and the Eiffel Tower in Paris, France.

▼ Just 240 visitors per day are allowed to climb the stairs to the Statue of Liberty's crown.

The Statue of Liberty

The Statue of Liberty stands on Liberty Island in New York Harbor. Before air travel, when people crossed the Atlantic Ocean by ship, it welcomed tourists and immigrants arriving in New York City. It was a gift to the USA from France as a monument to freedom and democracy. With its stone base, it stands 93 metres high. It was made of copper sheets fixed to an iron tower. The tower was connected to the copper skin by an **armature** – a flexible framework that let the skin move in strong winds without cracking. The statue was built in France in 1884, then taken apart and shipped to New York. It was reassembled on the stone base in 1886.

▲By the 1980s, the armature supporting the Statue of Liberty's skin had corroded and needed to be replaced.

MEGA FACTS

The sunlit side of the Eiffel Tower expands more than the shaded side, making the top of the tower lean up to 18 centimetres away from the Sun.

Masts and towers

In past centuries, towers were built as defensive structures or to hold church bells high above the ground. Even taller towers are built today for long-distance communications. Radio signals have to be broadcast over long distances. This is done by transmitters on top of tall masts or towers.

Radio masts

Radio masts are usually made of an open lattice. The lattice is lighter than solid metal and it lets the wind blow through it. Unlike tall buildings, radio masts do not have any **foundations** under the ground to hold them upright. Instead, they are held up by cables called **guys** or metal rods called **stays** – just like the ropes that hold up tents.

◄ *The KVLY-TV mast in North Dakota, USA, is the world's tallest mast. It is made of a 594-metre steel lattice mast with a 34-metre high transmitting antenna on top. When it was completed in 1963, it was the first artificial structure to exceed 609 metres.*

► *The Sky Tower in Auckland, New Zealand, is a concrete communications tower that can withstand winds of up to 200 kilometres per hour.*

Towers

Cities need radio antennae high above the ground because tall buildings often get in the way of radio and television signals. Radio masts may not be very pretty to look at, but they are usually located in remote places where their appearance does not matter. They are not suitable for use in cities because their guys and stays take up too much land. Sometimes, in cities, radio antennae are fixed to the tops of tall buildings, but if this is not possible, a communications tower is needed. Concrete towers are used, because they look better than masts and they are self-supporting – they do not need guys or stays to hold them up.

Tourist attractions

Concrete communications towers often have observation decks and restaurants near the top. The 553-metre CN Tower in Toronto, Canada, is the tallest concrete communications tower in the western hemisphere. At 328 metres, the Sky Tower in Auckland, New Zealand, is the tallest in the southern hemisphere. The world's tallest concrete communications tower is the Canton Tower in Guangzhou, China, which stands 610 metres high. It was completed in 2010 in time to relay television pictures of the Asian Games. It is made of an open steel lattice wrapped around a strong concrete core.

▶ *The Canton Tower in Guangzhou, China, contains radio and television transmitters, observation decks, revolving restaurants, shops and cinemas.*

MEGA FACTS

The KVLY-TV mast was built in 1963 in just 30 days. At 628 metres, it was the world's tallest artificial structure until Burj Khalifa was built.

The CN Tower

In the early 1970s, a number of skyscrapers were built in Toronto, Canada's biggest city. These new buildings made it difficult for people to receive radio and television programmes as they blocked the signal. The CN Tower was built in the middle of the city to broadcast signals from above the other buildings. It is one of the world's tallest towers. From the ground to the tip of its antenna, it stands 553 metres high.

What a view!

The CN Tower opened to the public in 1976. Up to 2 million people visit it every year. They travel up the tower in lifts and visit two levels called pods near the top – the Main Pod and an even higher Sky Pod. The Main Pod has a revolving restaurant that makes a complete rotation every 72 minutes. There are also observation decks giving breathtaking views across the city. Brave visitors to one of the observation decks can stand on a glass floor and see the ground 342 metres below their feet!

▲ On a clear day, the view from the top of the CN Tower stretches to the horizon more than 160 kilometres away.

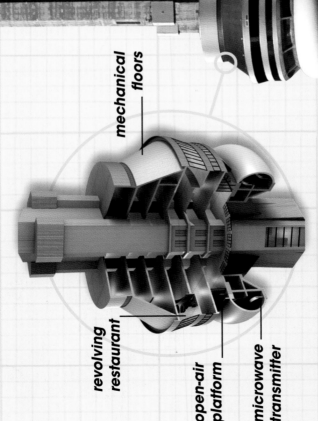

mechanical floors

revolving restaurant

open-air platform

microwave transmitter

height: 553 metres

Finishing off

The concrete construction work was completed by March 1975. The 102-metre steel antenna was lifted to the top in 44 pieces by a helicopter. The final section was bolted in place on 2 April 1975. The tower was opened to the public on 26 June 1976.

▲ *The tower's three-legged shape was produced by pouring concrete into a mould.*

Building a giant

Construction work began in 1973. Most of the tower is made from concrete with a tall steel mast on the top. A six-sided pillar in the middle is surrounded by three massive supporting legs. The legs hold the tower steady in the strongest winds.

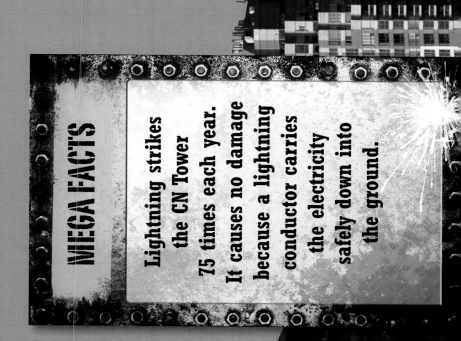

MEGA FACTS

Lightning strikes the CN Tower 75 times each year. It causes no damage because a lightning conductor carries the electricity safely down into the ground.

Offshore platforms

Offshore platforms stand in the sea and bring valuable oil and gas up from below the seabed. The part of an offshore platform that is above the waves is enormous, but the part that is under the sea is much, much bigger, and the whole structure is as tall as a skyscraper.

The tallest platforms are the ones that stand on the seabed on legs made of steel or concrete. Several decks of equipment and crew quarters, called the topsides, sit on top of the legs. The platform is towed out to sea and then tanks inside the legs are flooded so that they sink to the seabed. Only about 30 metres or so of the legs are visible above the waves.

▲ *Offshore oil platforms are made on land and then towed out to sea.*

Record breaker

The biggest and heaviest structure ever transported is the Troll A gas platform. It stands in the sea about 80 kilometres northwest of Bergen, Norway, bringing gas up from the Troll gas field. Its giant concrete legs are 369 metres high and weigh an astonishing 656,000 tonnes. Troll A was built in the sheltered waters of a Norwegian **fjord**. When the legs were completed, they were partly submerged so that the decks could be lifted on top. Then the whole structure, now 472 metres high, was towed out to its current position and sunk to the seabed. The massive legs buried themselves 35 metres into the soft mud.

▼ The Eiffel Tower was once the world's tallest man-made structure. The Troll A offshore platform is 160 metres taller.

◄ This oil platform is designed to drill in water depths of up to 3000 metres.

failures and accidents

Tall structures are designed to be safe and are built with great care, but sometimes something may go wrong. Although this is very rare, tall structures can suffer extraordinary accidents, failures and faults that their designers and builders had not anticipated. The tallest skyscrapers are covered with tens of thousands of windows. It is vital that they do not break or fall out. Large, heavy panels of glass falling from a skyscraper into the streets below could be lethal.

Falling windows

When the John Hancock Tower in Boston, USA, was built in the 1970s, it was covered with blue, mirrored glass. Soon after the windows were installed, they started crashing to the ground. Researchers found that the **solder** (a metal **alloy**) that filled the space between the glass and frame was too stiff. When the panels flexed in the wind, as they were designed to do, the solder cracked. This cracked the glass and the windows fell out.

▼ Dozens of radio masts have fallen down over the years. Most toppled in storms, while some were hit by aeroplanes. Others collapsed during maintenance work.

Safety first

It is important that workers use safe building methods to prevent serious accidents. On 27 June 2009, a nearly finished 13-storey apartment building in Shanghai, China, fell onto its side. An inquiry found that the problem was caused by workers digging a deep pit for an underground garage on one side of the building while also piling earth high on the other side. These earth movements unbalanced the ground so much that it gave way.

▲ This building in Shanghai, China, fell because of nearby digging. Its foundation piles stuck out of its base like the roots of an fallen tree.

Looking into the future

Architects, designers and engineers continue to develop skyscrapers and towers in shapes that have never been seen before. Some new designs for tall structures are driven by function. Others unashamedly seek the biggest 'wow' factor and the sharpest intake of breath from visitors.

The Gherkin

The 180-metre building in London, UK, called 30 St Mary Axe, better known as the 'Gherkin', is egg-shaped. The architects Norman Foster and Ken Shuttleworth gave it its curved shape in order to encourage the wind to flow around it. The wind is not deflected downwards, so the building does not create blasts of wind on the pavements below as other skyscrapers can.

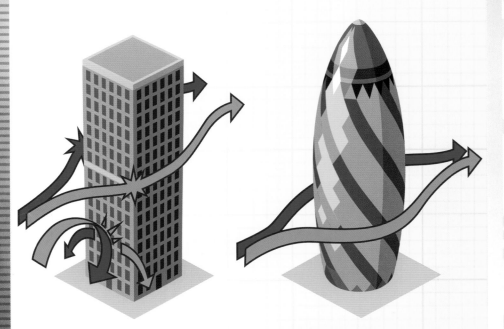

▲ *Skyscrapers with flat sides can deflect winds down onto pedestrians at street level. The Gherkin's shape allows wind to flow around it.*

▶ *The Capital Gate skyscraper in Abu Dhabi is supported by an external frame of diagonal supports, called a diagrid.*

Shaping up

Until recently, most skyscrapers were rectangular blocks. Now, more architects and engineers are exploring the possibilities of building skyscrapers in all sorts of different shapes. The 160-metre Capital Gate building in Abu Dhabi leans at a precarious angle of 18 degrees. Unlike the Leaning Tower of Pisa, the Capital Gate building was designed to have this distinctive lean. Its floors overhang each other from the 12th floor upwards.

Even stranger-looking skyscrapers are being planned. Future skyscrapers may change shape as their floors slowly rotate around the building's core. A 420-metre skyscraper like this is planned for Dubai. Each floor will rotate separately from all the others. The building's energy needs will be met by its own wind **turbines** and solar panels.

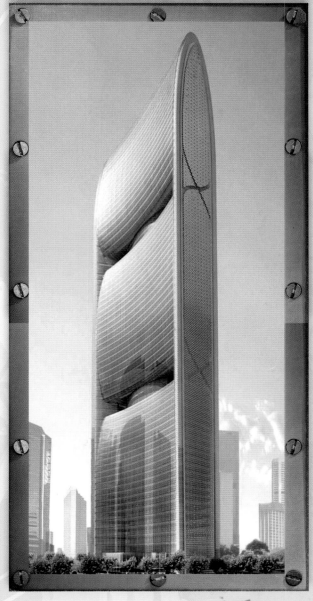

▼ **The Pearl River Tower in Guangzhou, China, lets air flow through it, powering wind turbines inside the building. The air is fed into the turbines through funnel-like openings in the building's walls.**

MEGA FACTS

The Pearl River Tower in Guangzhou, China, may be the first 'green' skyscraper. As well as wind turbines, it has solar panels and other green technology.

GIGANTIC LENGTHS AND OTHER VAST MEGASTRUCTURES

Top 10 Longest bridges and tunnels

Bridges	Location	Completed
Lake Pontchartrain Causeway	USA	1956, 1969
Manchac Swamp Bridge	USA	1970
Yangcun Bridge	China	2007
Hangzhou Bay Bridge	China	2007
Runyang Bridge	China	2005
Transport tunnels		
Seikan Tunnel	Japan	1988
Channel Tunnel	England-France	1994
Lötschberg Base Tunnel	Switzerland	2007
Guadarrama Railway Tunnel	Spain	2007
Iwate–Ichinohe Tunnel	Japan	2002

Over and under

Bridges and tunnels have been built since ancient times, but today they are bigger and longer than ever. These amazing engineering projects enable cars and other vehicles to take a more direct route across wide stretches of water or through the middle of mountains.

Building bridges

Bridges have developed from the simple ropes and vines that spanned rivers in prehistoric times to today's graceful steel and concrete structures that seem to defy gravity. The giant bridges built today are so long that they have to be shaped to fit the curve of the Earth's surface.

Tunnels

While bridges stand tall in the open for everyone to see, tunnels are hidden under the ground. The longest tunnels carry water into cities from distant **reservoirs**, but the most impressive tunnels are those through which we can travel: road and railway tunnels. The longest transport tunnel in use today is the Seikan Tunnel. This 54-kilometre railway tunnel links the Japanese islands of Honshu and Hokkaido under the sea.

MEGA FACTS

The 137-kilometre-long Delaware Aqueduct is the world's longest tunnel. It is part of a network that supplies New York City, USA, with water.

▲ The Bosphorus Bridge is a suspension bridge in Istanbul, Turkey. It links the continents of Europe and Asia.

► *The Ponte Vecchio, which spans the River Arno in Florence, Italy, was built in the 14th century. As was common with bridges at that time, it has shops along it.*

Particle smasher

There is a tunnel 175 metres under the border between France and Switzerland that does not lead anywhere. It goes round in a circle, 27 kilometres in circumference. The tunnel was built in the 1980s to house a scientific instrument called the Large Electron–Positron Collider. Subatomic particles were fired through a pipe inside the 3.8-metre-wide tunnel, and scientists studied what happened when they collided. Today, there is a new scientific instrument, the Large Hadron Collider, in the tunnel.

▲ *Particles hurtle around the Large Hadron Collider at close to the speed of light.*

► The Akashi Kaikyo Bridge in Japan is stiffened by metal beams linked together in triangles, creating a very strong structure.

Building long

Bridge and tunnel designers and engineers have to overcome several problems. For example, bridges have to cope with every type of weather, from blistering heat to freezing cold. Tunnels have to resist the crushing weight of the ground above them.

Stretching bridges

Materials grow bigger when they heat up. On a hot day, a bridge expands and becomes longer. Joints, called expansion joints, are built into the **roadway** of a bridge. They let the roadway grow longer without causing any damage. Arch-shaped bridges made from steel **girders** expand in length and height when they heat up. Hinges are built into the arch to let it expand.

MEGA FACTS

On a hot day, the steel arch of Sydney Harbour Bridge can expand and rise by up to 18 centimetres. Hinges at each end of the bridge let it rise and fall safely.

Resisting weight

When a long tunnel is dug, the weight of the ground above it will eventually squash it flat unless the tunnellers strengthen it. To keep a new tunnel in the right shape, it is lined with a strong, thick layer of reinforced concrete. Deep tunnels are usually circular as this shape is very strong.

The blinking bridge

▲ *Pedestrians walk across the bridge when the 'eye' is closed.*

▲ *The walkway tilts up to allow ships to pass underneath the bridge.*

Bridges are often built over busy shipping lanes. Low bridges may have sections that open to let boats through. The Gateshead Millennium Bridge over the River Tyne in England, UK, makes room for boats in an unusual way: the ends of the curved bridge stay attached to the river's banks while the rest of the bridge tilts up. Because of the way it opens, it is known as the 'Blinking Eye Bridge'.

How are they built?

The world's longest bridges and tunnels are huge projects. Whether engineers are planning to build a bridge or a tunnel, the first thing they do is find out what the ground is like. They bore holes in it and take samples to see what it is made of and how strong it is. Because bridges are very heavy, they must stand on solid rock, so bridge builders also need to know how far the **bedrock** is below the surface.

Bridge-building

Building a bridge begins with the construction of **piers**, the supports that hold up the bridge. Depending on what type of bridge it is, tall towers might have to be built on top of some of the piers to support cables that hold up the bridge's **deck**. A suspension bridge's cables are fixed at each end of the bridge to massive concrete blocks called **anchorages**. Next, the bridge's roadway, or deck, is lifted into position, section by section. A floating crane does this job for a low bridge over water, but the biggest bridges are too high for most floating cranes. For these bridges, hooks are lowered from the bridge itself to lift the bridge sections from barges in the water below.

▶ *Workers finish building the deck of the Hangzhou Bay Bridge, the world's longest sea bridge, near Shanghai, China, in 2007.*

► *The Millau Viaduct in France was built in a different way from most bridges. Half of the deck was built at each end of the bridge. Then the two halves were slid out onto the tops of supporting towers until they met in the middle.*

Tunnelling

Tunnellers need to know what sort of rock they are dealing with. Once they know, they can decide how to build the tunnel. One way is to use a **tunnel boring machine (TBM)**, which goes through the ground like a huge earthworm. A toothed disc, called the cutter head, on the front of a TBM rotates slowly, grinding away the rock. If the rocks are too hard for a TBM to cut, tunnellers use explosives instead. The rock shattered by the explosions is hauled out of the tunnel and the walls are lined with concrete.

▼ *A giant TBM is prepared for digging. Its service train stretches behind it.*

MEGA FACTS

Each of the concrete anchorages at the ends of the Golden Gate Bridge, San Fransisco, USA, weighs more than 54,000 tonnes — that is heavier than a battleship.

► The Golden Gate Bridge weighs 804,700 tonnes. This immense weight is held up by two main suspension cables, each made of 27,572 steel wires.

Famous giants

Some of the world's great bridges are so famous that they are instantly recognized. These bridges include the Golden Gate Bridge and Brooklyn Bridge in the USA and the Sydney Harbour Bridge in Australia.

The Golden Gate Bridge

The Golden Gate Bridge spans San Francisco Bay on the west coast of the USA. The bay was a difficult place to build a bridge because of its fast ocean currents, strong winds and the danger of earthquakes. When the Golden Gate Bridge was built in the 1930s, it was the world's longest suspension bridge. Its total length is 2.7 kilometres, while its main span is 1280 metres long. Most bridges are grey or silver-coloured, but the Golden Gate Bridge is painted a distinctive colour called International Airways Orange.

The Brooklyn Bridge

The Brooklyn Bridge links Brooklyn with Manhattan across New York City's East River. It was built between 1869 and 1883. The Brooklyn Bridge is a suspension bridge supported by two enormous **masonry** towers 486 metres apart. When the bridge opened, it carried a pair of railway tracks with roads on each side and a **footway** for pedestrians. The railway tracks were removed in 1944.

◄ *The Brooklyn Bridge was the first to have suspension cables made of steel. Until then, cables were made of iron.*

Sydney Harbour Bridge

Australia's Sydney Harbour Bridge is the world's biggest steel arch bridge. The two halves of the arch were built out from opposite sides of the harbour until they met in the middle. Then the deck was hung from the arch. The whole bridge is held together by 6 million rivets, which were all driven into place by hand. The bridge carries eight vehicle lanes, two railway tracks, a footway and a cycle lane.

◄ *The arch of the Sydney Harbour Bridge is 503 metres long and rises to a height of 134 metres.*

There had been plans for a bridge or tunnel across the estuary of the River Humber in northeast England, UK, since the 1870s, but work on the project did not finally begin until 1959. The first decision to be made was whether to build a bridge or a tunnel. A bridge was chosen because **geologists** found that the ground under the river was not suitable for tunnelling.

Spanning the estuary

The shifting sands in the estuary meant that the deep-water channel used by ships kept moving. Because of this, the bridge could not rest on a series of piers across the river, so it was decided to build a suspension bridge. Construction work on the bridge began in 1973. A pier was built at each side of the river and a concrete tower was built on top of each pier. The towers are 1410 metres apart, and the total length of the bridge is 2200 metres. The suspension cables were strung between massive concrete anchorages at each end of the bridge.

◄ *The bridge's towers are so tall that their tops sometimes peek out above the low clouds that settle over the river.*

◄ *The supporting tower on the north bank of the river starts to take shape one year into the bridge's construction.*

The Humber Bridge

length: 2200 metres

Laying the deck

The deck was built in steel sections 22 metres across – wide enough for four lanes of traffic. A 3-metre strip added to each side of the deck carries cycle tracks and footways. The deck was hoisted into position, section by section, and hung from the cables. The bridge was completed in 1981.

MEGA FACTS

Because of the curvature of the Earth's surface, the Humber Bridge's towers are 36 millimetres further apart at the top than at the bottom.

location: River Humber, Humberside, UK

The longest tunnels

Road and rail tunnels can cut hours off journey times by providing more direct routes through mountains. The longest tunnels include the Guadarrama Railway Tunnel in Spain and the Lötschberg Base Tunnel in Switzerland.

The train in Spain

In 2007, a new railway tunnel through the Guadarrama Mountains in Spain opened. The Guadarrama Railway Tunnel was Europe's fourth-longest rail tunnel. It was built to carry high-speed trains that run at up to 300 kilometres per hour. The twin-bore tunnel was carved out of the rock by four tunnel boring machines (TBMs). Two machines set out from the ends of the two tunnels towards each other. They were guided so accurately that they were only 10 centimetres out of line when they met. The TBMs bored two tunnels 9.5 metres across. The two tunnels are connected every 250 metres by cross-tunnels.

Through the Alps

▲ The two tubes of the tunnel are connected to each other every 333 metres, so each tunnel can be used as an emergency escape route for the other tunnel.

The Alps mountain range forms a natural barrier between Italy and the rest of Europe. Since the 1870s, more than a dozen tunnels have been dug through the mountains. In 2007, the Lötschberg Base Tunnel opened, cutting the journey time between Germany and Italy by a third. The ground was very difficult to cut through because it was made of hard rock. Some of the tunnel could be dug by TBMs, but most of it had to be blasted out with explosives.

Short and long

Bridges can be built using many different techniques depending on the length of the gap to be spanned and the kind of ground on which the bridge stands. Short bridges just a few metres long are usually built as simple beam bridges. Most of the longest bridges, some of them several kilometres long, are suspension bridges.

Beam

The simplest type of bridge is the **beam** bridge – a beam supported at each end. A tree trunk laid across a stream is a beam bridge, so beam bridges were probably the first bridges ever built. They are still used for bridging narrow gaps.

beam

Arch

An arch is a curved structure that spans a gap. It can support more weight than a beam bridge. The weight of an arch bridge tries to push the ends of the bridge apart. Massive blocks called **abutments** hold them in place.

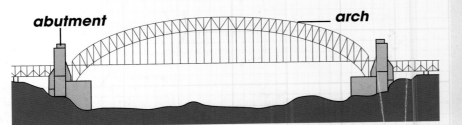

abutment   arch

In 1991, the governments of Sweden and Denmark agreed to build a link between their two countries. It was to cross a stretch of water called the Øresund **Strait**, connecting the Danish capital Copenhagen to the Swedish city of Malmö. The link was divided into two parts – a bridge and a tunnel. The tunnel was chosen for the Danish side of the crossing because a bridge with tall towers could have been a danger to low-flying aircraft near Copenhagen Airport.

Cable-stayed bridge

The Øresund Bridge stands on a line of concrete piers 140 metres apart. Once the piers were built, the bridge deck was lifted into position on top of them. Each 140-metre section of the deck weighed 6500 tonnes. The bridge has two decks, one above the other. Road traffic uses the upper deck and trains use the lower deck. The decks rise gently from each end to a height of 55 metres in the middle. There are no piers underneath the middle section so that ships can sail under it. This part of the bridge is held up by cables hanging from two tall towers called pylons. This is an example of a cable-stayed bridge.

▼ *The Øresund Bridge has the world's longest cable-stayed main span at 1092 metres.*

The Øresund Link

total length: 16·4 kilometres   bridge le

MEGA FACTS

During construction of the Øresund Link, workers found 16 unexploded bombs on the seabed. The bombs had been dropped during World War II (1939–45).

Peberholm Island

The bridge and tunnel meet at an artificial island called Peberholm. It was made from sand, stone and mud **dredged** from the seabed. More than 7.5 million cubic metres of seabed had to be dug up. That is enough to fill 3000 Olympic-size swimming pools.

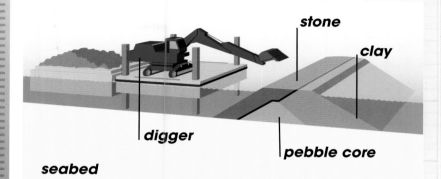

stone

clay

digger

pebble core

seabed

▲ The dyke (wall) built around Peberholm Island was covered with stone to protect it from damage caused by waves.

double-decker bridge carries cars (above) and trains (below)

▶ Machines called roadheaders are used to dig tunnels that are too small and short for TBMs.

◀ Because TBMs are so big, they are usually assembled and taken apart deep underground.

MEGA FACTS

When it was completed in October 2010, the 56-kilometre-long Gotthard Base Tunnel in the Alps became the world's longest railway tunnel.

Cantilever

A **cantilever** is a beam held up at one end only, like a shelf. One way to build a cantilever bridge is to build decks out from both sides of a tower so that they balance each other. The two parts of the deck are the cantilevers.

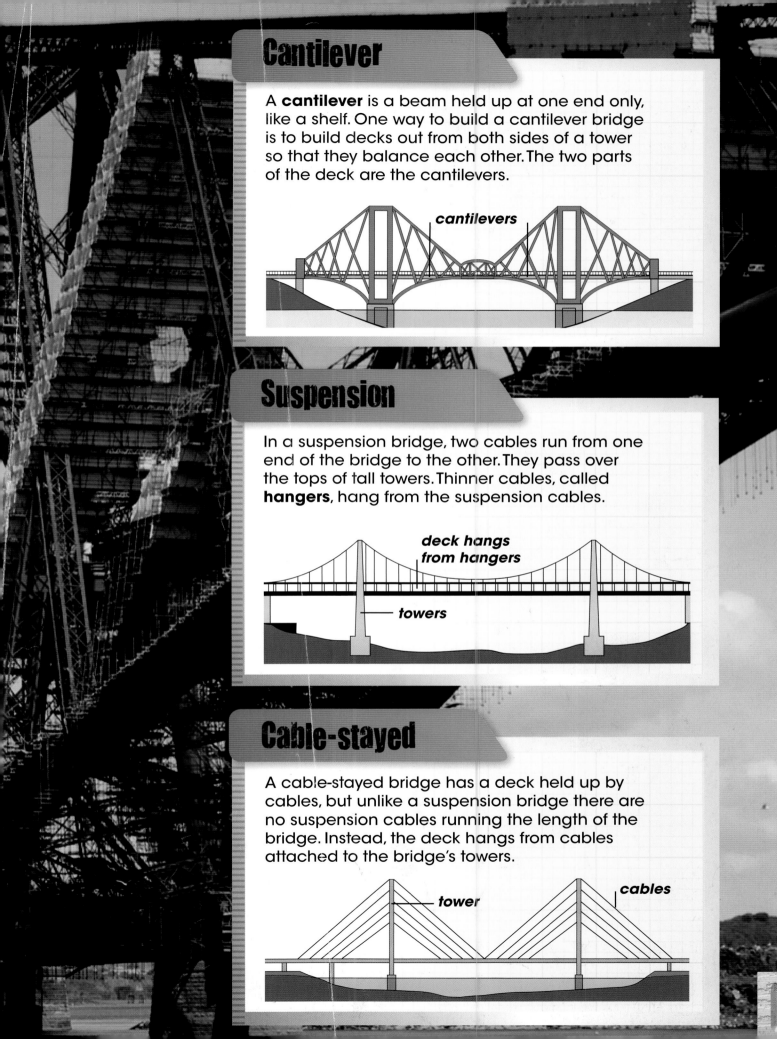

cantilevers

Suspension

In a suspension bridge, two cables run from one end of the bridge to the other. They pass over the tops of tall towers. Thinner cables, called **hangers**, hang from the suspension cables.

*deck hangs
from hangers*

towers

Cable-stayed

A cable-stayed bridge has a deck held up by cables, but unlike a suspension bridge there are no suspension cables running the length of the bridge. Instead, the deck hangs from cables attached to the bridge's towers.

tower

cables

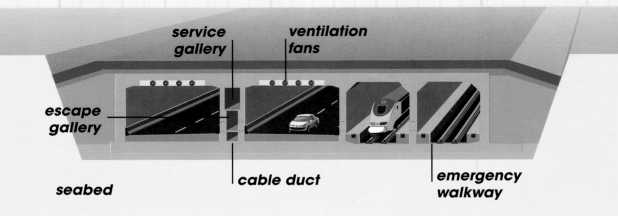

▲ The tunnel carries two two-lane roadways and two railway tracks inside four side-by-side galleries. In case of emergencies, there is an escape tunnel between the roadways and walkways alongside the railway tracks.

Royal opening

The first vehicle drove through the tunnel in March 1999. In 2000, Queen Margrethe II of Denmark and King Carl XVI Gustaf of Sweden opened the completed bridge–tunnel link to the public. Every year, more than 25 million people cross the Øresund Link, including 15 million travelling by car and more than 10 million by train. In December 2010, the City Tunnel, a 17-kilometre rail link from the Øresund Link to Malmö Central Station, was opened. It carries passengers under the streets of Malmö to the centre of the city.

opened: 2000

◄ *The tunnel sits in a trench dug into the seabed. In total, it weighs 1.1 million tonnes, equivalent to the weight of 10 large cruise ships.*

Tunnel to Denmark

The tunnel was made in sections in a factory built specially for the job. The tunnel sections were made from concrete. Each section was enormous, measuring 176 metres long, 9 metres high and 40 metres wide, and weighing 55,000 tonnes. One by one, 20 of these sections were floated out to the right position and then lowered from barges into a trench dug in the seabed. When they were in position, they were connected. Then the tunnel was covered with mud and clay from the seabed to weigh it down and protect it from being hit by a ship or a ship's anchor.

location: Øresund Strait between Denmark and Sweden

The hazard factor

Bridges and tunnels face a number of **hazards**, from traffic accidents to extreme weather. They are constantly monitored to check for any damage or decay and to make sure they remain safe.

Cold comfort

Icy roads are often treated with salt to melt the ice. The salty water this produces can sink down into a bridge's concrete roadway and rust the steel bars inside the concrete. Steel expands when it rusts. If the steel bars inside concrete rust, they expand and crack the concrete.

Forces of nature

Deep underground, tunnels are protected from the storms that can damage bridges, but they may be destroyed by **earthquakes** that move the ground. Tunnels are carefully checked for damage after every quake.

▲ When an earthquake shook Sweden on 16 December 2008, technicians checked the Drogden Tunnel to make sure it had not been damaged. They did this by measuring the distance between fixed points to check that they had not moved.

► The I-10 Bridge in Florida, USA, was damaged by Hurricane Ivan in 2004. More than 100 sections were pushed out of place or collapsed altogether.

Falling ice

Cold weather can produce other dangers to traffic on a bridge. Ice can build up on the bridge's cables and **gantries** until chunks big enough to smash a car windscreen crash to the ground. Bridges may have to close if falling ice makes them too dangerous to cross.

Pinging cables

Some suspension bridges suffer from a problem that weakens their suspension cables. If moisture gets in between the steel wires that make up the massive cables, the wires rust. Within a few years, they start breaking. If this continues unchecked, year after year, the bridge will eventually become dangerously weak. Microphones attached to the cables pick up the pinging sounds made by the breaking wires. One way to stop the problem getting any worse is to pump dry air through the cables to drive out the moisture. This process is called dehumidification.

▼ The cables that hold up the Forth Road Bridge in Scotland, UK, wrap around holders, called yokes, in concrete chambers. The cables are regularly inspected for damage.

Monster spans

China's Hangzhou Bay Bridge and Portugal's Vasco da Gama Bridge are among the world's longest bridges. The Hangzhou Bay Bridge is the world's longest bridge over sea, while the Vasco da Gama Bridge is Europe's longest bridge.

China's record-breaker

The 36-kilometre-long Hangzhou Bay Bridge links China's most populous city, Shanghai, with the city of Ningbo. The bridge crosses Hangzhou Bay, part of the East China Sea, an area with strong currents that is regularly battered by tropical storms. Most of the bridge is made of short spans sitting on top of piers anchored to the seabed, but two parts of the bridge are higher than the rest and are held up by cables hanging from towers. These cable-stayed spans have no supports below the deck, which means that ships can sail underneath them.

MEGA FACTS

Nearly 600 experts worked for nine years on the design of the Hangzhou Bay Bridge, because it was to be built in such a difficult place for a bridge.

▲ *The Hangzhou Bay Bridge carries a six-lane highway across the sea. It opened in 2008 and is designed to last for 100 years.*

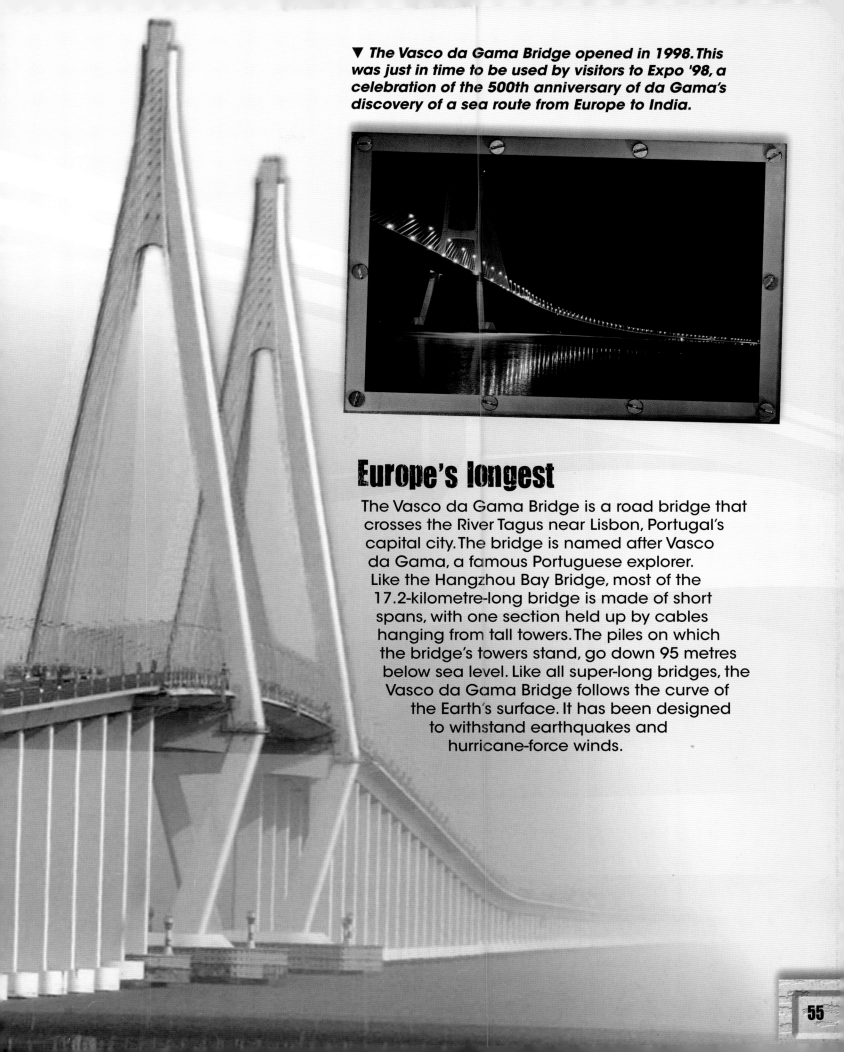

▼ *The Vasco da Gama Bridge opened in 1998. This was just in time to be used by visitors to Expo '98, a celebration of the 500th anniversary of da Gama's discovery of a sea route from Europe to India.*

Europe's longest

The Vasco da Gama Bridge is a road bridge that crosses the River Tagus near Lisbon, Portugal's capital city. The bridge is named after Vasco da Gama, a famous Portuguese explorer. Like the Hangzhou Bay Bridge, most of the 17.2-kilometre-long bridge is made of short spans, with one section held up by cables hanging from tall towers. The piles on which the bridge's towers stand, go down 95 metres below sea level. Like all super-long bridges, the Vasco da Gama Bridge follows the curve of the Earth's surface. It has been designed to withstand earthquakes and hurricane-force winds.

The Lake Pontchartrain Causeway in Louisiana, USA, is the world's longest bridge over water. From end to end, it measures 38.4 kilometres. It is so long that, because of the curved shape of the Earth's surface, someone standing at one end of the bridge cannot see the other end. The causeway spans Lake Pontchartrain, the second-biggest saltwater lake in the USA. The city of New Orleans lies on the lake's south shore.

Twin bridges

The causeway is actually two bridges side by side. The first bridge was finished in 1956. It proved so popular that within 10 years, more than 3000 vehicles were using it every day. A second bridge was built alongside. It opened in 1969. The bridges are linked together at seven points, so that traffic can cross from one bridge to the other in an emergency. There are also drawbridges, called **bascules**, that open to let boats through.

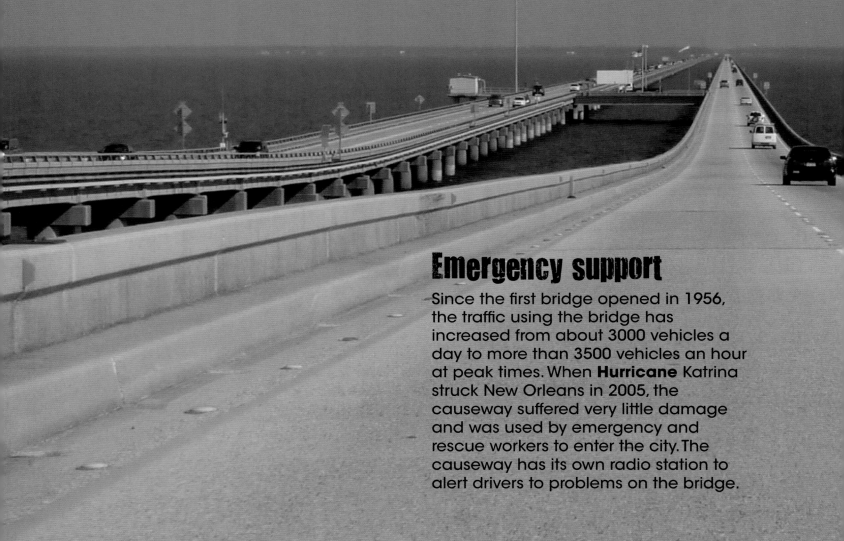

Emergency support

Since the first bridge opened in 1956, the traffic using the bridge has increased from about 3000 vehicles a day to more than 3500 vehicles an hour at peak times. When **Hurricane** Katrina struck New Orleans in 2005, the causeway suffered very little damage and was used by emergency and rescue workers to enter the city. The causeway has its own radio station to alert drivers to problems on the bridge.

Lake Pontchartrain Causeway

length: 38.4 kilometres

◄ A bascule opens to let boats through. Fenders protect the bridge from bumps by boats as they pass through. A radar system alerts officials if a boat comes within 1.6 kilometres of the bridge.

▼ The twin spans of the Lake Pontchartrain Causeway disappear over the horizon. Driving at 115 kilometres per hour, it takes more than 20 minutes to cross the bridge.

MEGA FACTS

The Lake Pontchartrain Causeway is so long that it spans one-thousandth of the Earth's circumference.

Subways

Railway systems that snake through a network of underground tunnels are called subways. They can move passengers across a busy city very quickly because the trains are not held up by heavy traffic or bad weather on the surface.

The first subway tunnels were built using the 'cut and cover' method. First, a large trench was dug down the middle of a street. Then the street was rebuilt on top of the tunnel. Today, subway tunnels may be more than 60 metres below the surface, and they are usually dug using tunnel boring machines (TBMs).

6 CARS – BOARD
PLATFORM 1

New York Subway

TBMs have become much more powerful over the years. The machine that is digging the new Second Avenue line in New York City, USA, is as powerful as 12 jumbo jets and can grind its way through 18 metres of rock a day. It was manufactured in about 1980 and has been used on at least four other projects. This latest subway line is due to open in 2016.

▲ *This tunnel boring machine was used during the construction of subway lines in New York City in the 1930s.*

Going electric

London was the first city in the world to have an underground railway. The first section, the Metropolitan line, opened in 1863. Today, there are 11 lines with routes covering more than 400 kilometres. The Northern line is the deepest line: in places it is 70 metres below ground. Electric trains were used from the beginning because they did not produce choking fumes like steam engines did.

► Flooding is a problem in subway networks. More than 30 million litres of water a day are pumped out of the London Underground.

▲ The subway system for San Francisco, known as the BART, has a WiFi system that allows passengers to access the Internet from the trains.

Failures and accidents

Engineers understand the forces that act on tunnels and bridges, but these enormous structures can sometimes surprise them. Accidents can happen to even the best-designed structures. Bridge designers try to make their bridges flexible enough to soak up small movements caused by strong winds and traffic, but stiff enough to stand safely for many years.

The wobbly bridge

When the Millennium Bridge, a footbridge across the River Thames in London, UK, opened in 2000, it swayed so much that it was nicknamed the 'Wobbly Bridge'. The problem was caused by something called synchronous lateral excitation. When people walked on the bridge, their footsteps made it sway a little from side to side. As soon as people felt this movement, they could not help walking in time with it, which made the swaying even worse. The bridge was closed while devices called dampers were fitted to fix the swaying.

▶ *The cables that hold up London's Millennium Bridge run along the sides rather than hanging above it.*

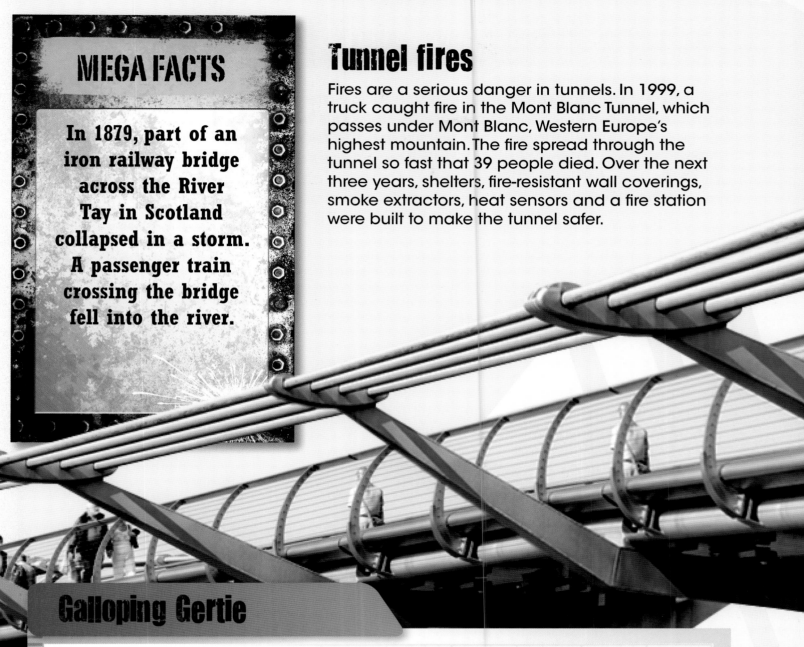

Tunnel fires

Fires are a serious danger in tunnels. In 1999, a truck caught fire in the Mont Blanc Tunnel, which passes under Mont Blanc, Western Europe's highest mountain. The fire spread through the tunnel so fast that 39 people died. Over the next three years, shelters, fire-resistant wall coverings, smoke extractors, heat sensors and a fire station were built to make the tunnel safer.

Galloping Gertie

When a suspension bridge across the Tacoma Narrows Strait in Washington state, USA, opened on 1 July 1940, it moved about so much in the wind that it was nicknamed 'Galloping Gertie'. Four months later, the bridge twisted to and fro so violently that it broke up. The collapse was caused by something called aeroelastic flutter. When the bridge started moving in the wind, its bendiness let it twist back and forth until it shook itself to bits.

◀ *The roadway of the Tacoma Narrows Bridge hangs in shreds. A wind of only 64 kilometres per hour made the bridge twist so much that it tore itself apart.*

Future bridges and tunnels

The longest bridges and tunnels in use today are marvels of engineering, but even longer transport links are being planned. Some of these are bridges that will smash the records set by today's bridges. Many of the world's new bridges will be built in East Asia. In particular, China is now a wealthy country that wants to make it easier for businesses to move people, materials and products between its cities and ports.

Bering Bridge

One of the most daring plans is for a bridge to link Russia and the USA across the Bering Strait. The bridge could carry a roadway, rail tracks and pipelines for oil and gas. Three bridges will be needed to span the strait – one from Russia to the Diomede Islands, one between the islands, and a third from the islands to Alaska, USA. Two of the three bridges will have to be longer than China's Hangzhou Bay Bridge – the longest sea bridge in the world today.

▲ *A bridge across the Bering Strait would be 88 kilometres long in total, passing over the Diomede Islands that lie halfway across the strait.*

Crossing the River Pearl

The Hong Kong–Zhuhai–Macao Bridge in China will be 50 kilometres long, with 35 kilometres of it over the sea. This massive project includes an underwater tunnel, two artificial islands and a series of bridges. Today, it takes about three hours to cross the River Pearl from Zhuhai or Macao to Hong Kong. The new link will cut this to 30 minutes when it opens in 2016.

The Fehmarn Belt Bridge

By 2018, cars and trains may be able to travel from Denmark to Germany across a bridge or through a tunnel. The decision is due to be made in 2013. If a bridge is chosen, the 20-kilometre-long link, called the Fehmarn Belt Bridge, will have a motorway and two railway tracks. Today, the journey takes about an hour by ferry, but with a bridge, the journey time would be slashed to 15 minutes.

▼ *The Fehmarn Belt Bridge will have two decks, one above the other. One will be for road traffic and the other for trains.*

MEGA FACTS

A bridge across the Bering Strait would stand on 220 piers built in icy water and strengthened to protect them from the impact of icebergs.

MASSIVE MONSTERS AND OTHER HUGE MEGASTRUCTURES

Top 10 biggest stadiums by capacity

Stadium	Location	Capacity
May Day Stadium	Pyongyang, North Korea	150,000
Salt Lake Stadium	Kolkata, India	120,000
Aztec Stadium	Mexico City, Mexico	115,000
Michigan Stadium	Michigan, USA	109,901
Beaver Stadium	Pennsylvania, USA	107,283
Neyland Stadium	Tennessee, USA	102,455
Ohio Stadium	Ohio, USA	102,329
Bryant–Denny Stadium	Alabama, USA	101,821
Darrell K Royal Stadium	Texas, USA	100,119

Building big

People have been building massive structures for thousands of years. The biggest structures built today include dams and artificial islands. The most familiar giant structures are sports **stadiums**, which are built in cities where millions of people can see and visit them.

Holding water

Dams are barriers built across rivers and other bodies of water. When a river is blocked by a dam, the water rises behind it to form a large lake called a reservoir. The water pushes against the dam with a huge force, so dams have to be heavy and strong to hold back the water. A reservoir supplies fresh water to the surrounding region. Large dams also work as power stations. Water from the reservoir flows through turbines inside the dam. This makes the turbines spin, driving **generators** that produce **hydroelectricity**.

MEGA FACTS

The world's biggest sports stadium is the May Day Stadium in Pyongyang, the capital city of North Korea. It can hold 150,000 spectators.

◀ The Cowboys Stadium, home of Dallas Cowboys American Football team, in Arlington, Texas, is the biggest domed stadium. It opened in 2009 and can seat 80,000 spectators.

Looking good

Fantastic new stadiums are built for major sports competitions such as the Olympic Games and football World Cup. Stadiums are designed by architects to be thrilling and exciting places to watch sport alongside thousands of other people. They have to look good on the outside and create a great experience for spectators inside. Even the way the sound of cheering spectators echoes around a stadium is an important part of the design.

▼ *China's Three Gorges Dam is the world's biggest hydroelectric power plant. The dam is 2.3 kilometres long and spans the Yangtze River.*

Building islands

Not all of the world's biggest man-made objects are buildings. Most of the thousands of islands dotted around the world were carved out by nature. However, a handful were built by people. Artificial islands are built to create more land for building. Homes, hotels, holiday resorts and even airports are built on artificial islands.

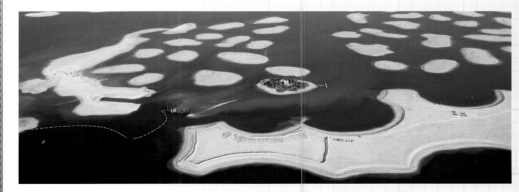

▲ *Built off the coast of Dubai, UAE, The World is a group of artificial islands that resembles a map of the world.*

Weighty designs

Massive structures weigh tens of thousands of tonnes. Building such big and heavy structures is difficult. The designers have to find the right places to build them, and to ensure that they will not collapse. Long before one of these structures is built, computers analyse its design, searching for weak points.

Bearing the weight

A big, heavy structure has to stand on firm ground that can bear its weight. Sometimes this presents difficulties. For example, the place chosen to build the Aztec Stadium in Mexico City was covered with volcanic rock. This rock was full of holes and criss-crossed with cracks. It was too weak to bear the 109,000-tonne stadium. About 180,000 tonnes of volcanic rock had to be removed to get down to solid bedrock on which to build the stadium.

▶ *A computer-generated image of a new stadium design shows fans and planning officials how it will look.*

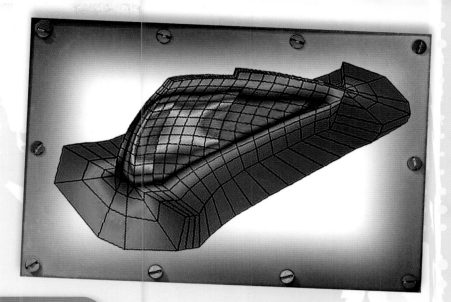

► *This computer model of an arch dam is colour-coded to show the strength of the forces acting upon it. The red blocks show the greatest forces and any potential weak spots.*

Flooding valleys

When new dams are built to create reservoirs, the valleys that are flooded by the rising water are not always empty. The bigger the reservoir, the more likely it is that people are already living on the land that will disappear under water. More than 1 million people had to be moved from 1000 towns and villages that were later submerged by the water rising behind China's Three Gorges Dam.

When the Aswan Dam was built across the Nile River in Egypt, the rising water would have submerged a pair of 3000-year-old temples at Abu Simbel. To save the temples, they were cut up into more than 1000 blocks and rebuilt on higher ground.

▲ *The Abu Simbel temples in Egypt were relocated when the Aswan Dam was built in the 1960s.*

MEGA FACTS

Mexico City's Aztec Stadium was built in 1966. The football World Cup final was held there in 1970 and 1986. Inside, there is room for 115,000 people.

Monster problems

Once a massive structure is built, it is constantly monitored and inspected to make sure there are no problems. Engineers look for cracks in large concrete structures. Cracks could mean that the ground is moving or sinking. Massive structures are so heavy that their weight can cause problems too.

Storm shelter

When Hurricane Katrina hit New Orleans, USA, in August 2005, high winds peeled off the rubber outer covering of the roof of the Louisiana Superdome. However, the stadium's strong concrete structure held firm, and it was used to shelter more than 30,000 people whose homes had been blown or washed away by the storm.

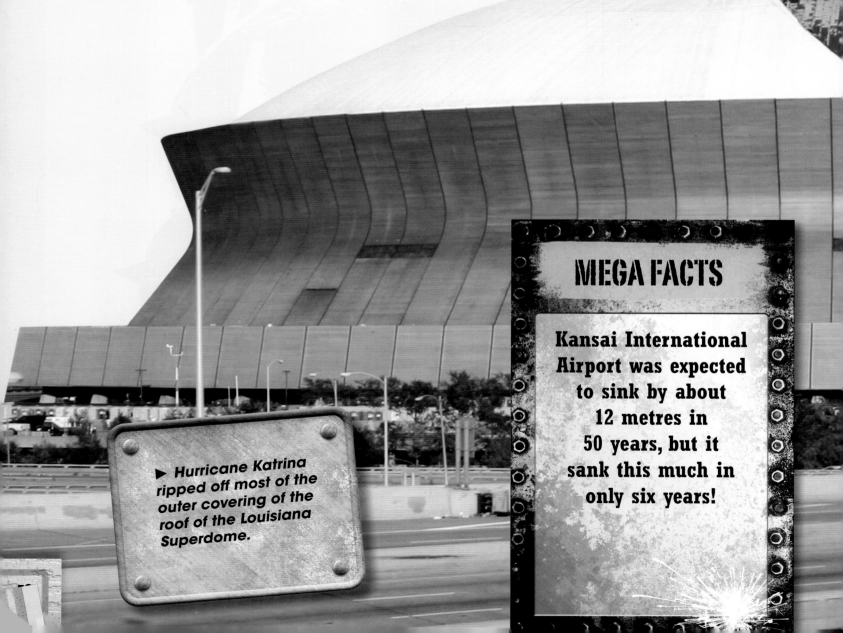

► Hurricane Katrina ripped off most of the outer covering of the roof of the Louisiana Superdome.

MEGA FACTS

Kansai International Airport was expected to sink by about 12 metres in 50 years, but it sank this much in only six years!

Causing quakes

Some structures are so heavy that they can cause earthquakes. Earthquakes happen because the thin crust of rock that forms the Earth's surface is cracked into pieces called plates. The plates rub against each other and get stuck. When they suddenly slip past each other, they can cause an earthquake. The weight of a dam or the reservoir behind it can set off small earthquakes called **tremors**. China's Three Gorges Dam and its reservoir have caused tremors strong enough to crack nearby roads and buildings.

▼ Cracks have appeared in many houses near the Three Gorges Dam following earthquakes caused by the giant structure.

Kansai Airport

Massive structures built on artificial islands face additional problems. When earth is piled up to make an artificial island, air is trapped between the particles of soil. Over time, the air is squeezed out, the particles squash closer together and the ground sinks. Kansai Airport in Japan was built on an artificial island. The designers of its terminal building knew it might sink unevenly. They solved the problem by standing the building on 900 pillars, which can be jacked up as land sinks.

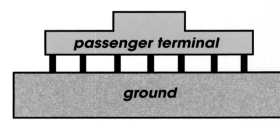

passenger terminal

ground

pillars

jack

▲ If the ground under Kansai Airport's passenger terminal sinks unevenly, it can be jacked up until it is level again.

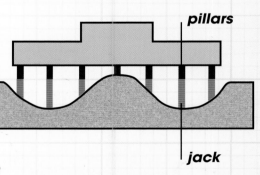

▼ Construction workers pour concrete into a reinforced structure of metal bars.

How are they built?

Building a huge, heavy structure is a difficult task that requires careful planning. Architects work closely with the engineers and technicians who turn their design into a real building.

Getting the land ready

Once a structure has been designed, the next job is to prepare the ground. Old buildings might have to be cleared away. Loose rock that cannot be built on must be removed and the ground levelled before construction can begin.

▼ Construction workers pour concrete into a reinforced structure of metal bars.

▲ Once the foundations of the Soccer City Stadium in Johannesburg, South Afica, were completed, its skeletonlike frame was built.

Building strength

▲ *The Bird's Nest Stadium was designed to withstand earthquakes.*

The Bird's Nest Stadium in Beijing, China, is made of a network of steel beams. It reached its full strength only when it was complete. The stadium was supported by 78 temporary columns while it was being built. When it was completed, the columns were removed.

Building methods

How a building is constructed depends on the type of structure. A concrete dam is built by pouring concrete into a mould. Concrete is very strong in compression (when it is squeezed), but it cracks easily when it is bent or stretched. To strengthen the concrete, it is poured over steel rods called reinforcing bars, or rebars. The concrete sets hard around them. This is called reinforced concrete.

Foundations

Some structures are so big and heavy that their weight is enough to keep them in position. The biggest and heaviest dams work like this. But most structures have to be anchored securely to the ground so that they do not move, sag or twist. They stand on underground pillars called piles. The piles provide a firm foundation for the building.

MEGA FACTS

China's Bird's Nest Stadium was built from 7500 steel beams. No two beams were alike. Each one was designed separately to ensure that they all fitted together.

Famous giants

The biggest structures of the Ancient World were pyramids, stadiums, tombs and temples. The heaviest and most impressive of all was the Great Pyramid of Khufu. The Colosseum in Rome was probably the world's first great stadium, and could hold 50,000 spectators. Today, the biggest structure of all is an airport terminal.

The biggest pyramids

The Great Pyramid of Khufu was built as a tomb for the Egyptian Pharaoh Khufu around 4500 years ago. It weighs nearly 6 million tonnes and is the heaviest man-made structure on Earth, but it is not the biggest. The Great Pyramid of Cholula in Mexico is bigger. Today, it looks like a natural hill, but it was once a grand stone pyramid.

▲ *The Great Pyramid of Khufu (above right) is one of a trio of pyramids built at Giza, Egypt.*

▶ *The Colosseum's arena measures 76 metres by 44 metres – about half the size of a football pitch. Its wood and stone floor was covered with sand.*

The Colosseum

The Colosseum was the Roman Empire's biggest **amphitheatre**, built to entertain people. The entertainment was often violent, including public executions and fights between gladiators. The Colosseum was constructed more than 1900 years ago. It is an oval building, 188 metres long, 156 metres wide and 48.5 metres high. It was built from limestone, bricks, concrete and volcanic rock.

▶ *Terminal 3 at Dubai International Airport covers the same area as 280 football fields.*

Modern marvel

In terms of floor space, the biggest building today is Terminal 3 of Dubai International Airport, UAE. It has 1.5 million square metres of floor space, and was built from enough concrete to fill 950 Olympic-size swimming pools. The concrete was reinforced by 450,000 tonnes of steel and a further 33,000 tonnes of steel were used to build the supporting structure.

MEGA FACTS

For 3800 years, the Great Pyramid of Khufu, at 139 metres high, was the tallest building in the world. The record was taken from it in 1311 by Lincoln Cathedral, UK.

Sydney Opera House stands on a plot of land jutting out into Sydney Harbour, surrounded on three sides by water. It was designed by the Danish architect Jørn Utzon, who won a competition in the 1950s to find the best design. Utzon's winning design resembled a set of curved shells nestling inside each other.

Running late

Construction of the Opera House began in 1959, and was expected to take about four years. However, its unique shape posed a series of tricky engineering problems. It finally opened 10 years late and 14 times over budget.

▶ The Opera House appears to float on the waters of Sydney Harbour. The ground it covers is big enough to park four jumbo jets.

Sydney Opera House

year completed: 1973   length: 185 metres

Sports stadiums

Sports stadiums are among the biggest and most impressive buildings constructed today. Each stadium is a one-off, specially designed for its home city. A stadium is a status symbol for the city, as well as being a functional building, where spectators can enjoy their favourite sport.

Clear view

Every spectator wants to have a clear view of every part of the playing surface or running track. Pillars would spoil their view – but without pillars, how does the roof stay up? The solution is to hold it up from above, hanging it from cables or metal struts. In most stadiums, the roof covers only the spectators, not the playing surface.

Domes

In parts of the world where storms are common, such as the southern states of the USA, stadiums may have to be completely covered during sports events to keep out extreme weather. In the 1960s and 1970s, stadiums covered with a domed roof were built. These roofs did not open at all.

▲ *The Houston Astrodome, which opened in 1965, was the world's first domed stadium.*

MEGA FACTS

The Allianz Arena (above) in Munich, Germany, is covered with plastic panels that can be lit up in different colours.

When London was awarded the 2012 Olympic Games in 2005, a seven-year countdown began. When the clock reaches zero, in July 2012, the Games begin. By then, London's new Olympic stadium has to be designed, built and tested. The design was unveiled in November 2007. It showed a bowl-shaped stadium partly sunk into the ground. The chosen site was an island between rivers in Stratford in northeast London.

Firm foundations

Construction of the 80,000-seat stadium began in April 2008. More than 800,000 tonnes of soil were removed from the site, and the first of 4000 piles, each 25 metres deep, was sunk into the ground to form a solid foundation. The ground at one end of the stadium is higher than the other end. This slope was used in the stadium's design. Athletes' changing rooms, treatment rooms, offices and facilities for the world's journalists and broadcasters were hidden underground at the end of the stadium where the ground is higher.

▼ *By September 2010, the basic structure of the stadium was complete. The lighting towers had been installed. Work on the field had begun.*

London's Olympic Stadium

capacity: 80,000   height: 53 metres

Taking shape

Concrete was laid to make the base of the bowl and the floor of the lower **tier** of seats. More than 100 columns, each 5 metres high, were built to support the stadium's structure. The lower seating tier contains 25,000 seats. The upper structure contains a higher tier of 55,000 seats. A fabric curtain surrounds the stadium and provides extra protection for the spectators from the weather. Above the spectators' heads, a 28-metre wide roof made of lightweight plastic fabric is held up by cables. Above the roof are 14 lighting towers.

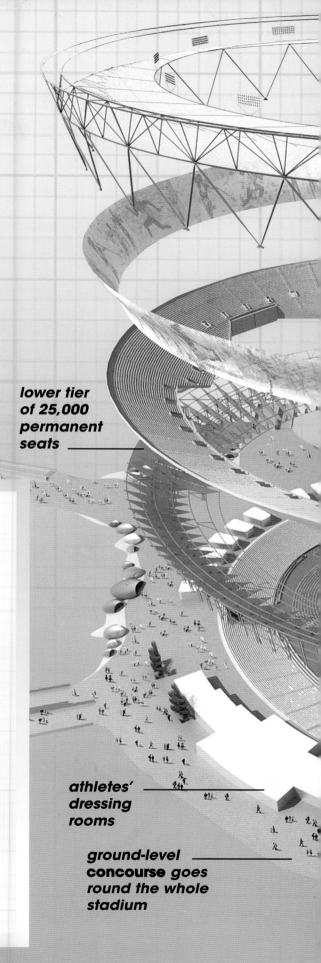

lower tier of 25,000 permanent seats _____

athletes' _____ dressing rooms

ground-level _____ concourse *goes round the whole stadium*

Steel skeleton

By 2009, cranes towered over the construction site of the Olympic Stadium. **Tower cranes** and mobile cranes worked together to lift the steel skeleton into position.

▲ *In November 2009, the concrete bowl that forms the base of the stadium was almost complete.*

Concert halls

The Opera House is 185 metres long and 120 metres wide. It has two main auditoriums (theatres) and three smaller ones. The largest auditorium holds more than 2650 people.

Construction

The building was constructed in three stages. Stage one involved building the foundations with a vast concrete platform on top. A total of 580 concrete piers were driven into the harbour floor. Stage two involved building the shell-like roofs. These were made from 2194 concrete sections weighing up to 15.5 tonnes each. It took eight years to design and build the roofs. Stage three involved finishing the interior of the building.

▲ *The Opera House nears completion in 1971. The concrete piers that bear its weight are visible underneath it.*

MEGA FACTS

Sydney Opera House uses 20 gigawatt hours of electricity a year – as much as a town of 25,000 people.

Green grass

Most stadiums have a playing surface made of grass. The grass needs plenty of light to keep it green and healthy, but a roof cuts down the amount of light reaching the grass. Even a roof that covers only the spectators cuts down the sunlight. One answer is to make part of the roof able to move. A movable roof can cover spectators during bad weather, but between events it can be opened up to let in more light. The roof on the south side of Wembley Stadium, London, UK, slides back to let more light onto the pitch.

▲ The arch that holds up Wembley Stadium's roof weighs 1750 tonnes – as much as 500 fully-laden trucks.

Setting records

The roof reduces wind speeds inside the stadium. This is important, because world records in some events can be set only if the wind is below a certain speed. The designers tested models of the stadium with wind blowing from different directions to measure the wind speeds at ground level.

▲ The stadium has been designed to hold all the track and field events in addition to the opening and closing ceremonies.

▲ The stadium is designed as a series of layers and rings one above the other, from the foundations up to the lighting towers.

cost: UK£537 million   completed: 2012

In the 1920s, the US government decided to build a dam across the Colorado River on the border of Arizona and Nevada. It was to be a massive, concrete arch-gravity dam.

Diverting the river

First, the course of the Colorado River had to be changed so that it flowed around the part of the river bed where the dam was to be built. This was done by blasting four tunnels through the walls of the Black Canyon.

The first concrete was poured in June 1933. The dam could not be made in one seamless block, because the concrete would have cracked as it set. Instead, the concrete was poured into moulds that formed blocks up to 15 metres square and 1.5 metres high. The blocks contained pipes. Chilled water was pumped through the pipes to make the concrete set more slowly and evenly to avoid cracking. Then the pipes were filled with **grout**. The vast concrete wall of the dam was finished in May 1935.

◄ The curved wall of the Hoover Dam seen here before Lake Mead had been created. The whole dam weighs nearly 6 million tonnes.

The Hoover Dam

length: 379 metres   height: 201 metres

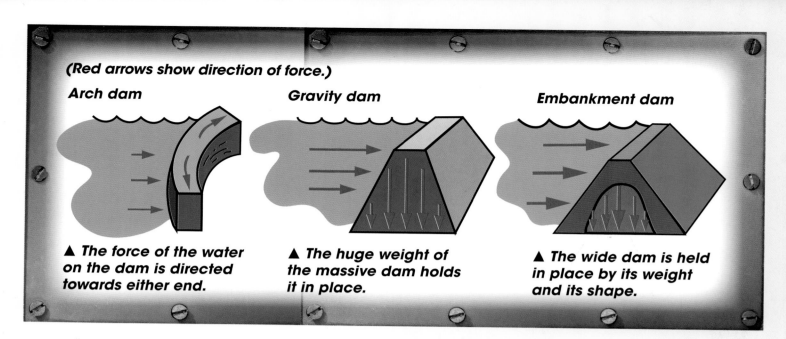

(Red arrows show direction of force.)

Arch dam

▲ The force of the water on the dam is directed towards either end.

Gravity dam

▲ The huge weight of the massive dam holds it in place.

Embankment dam

▲ The wide dam is held in place by its weight and its shape.

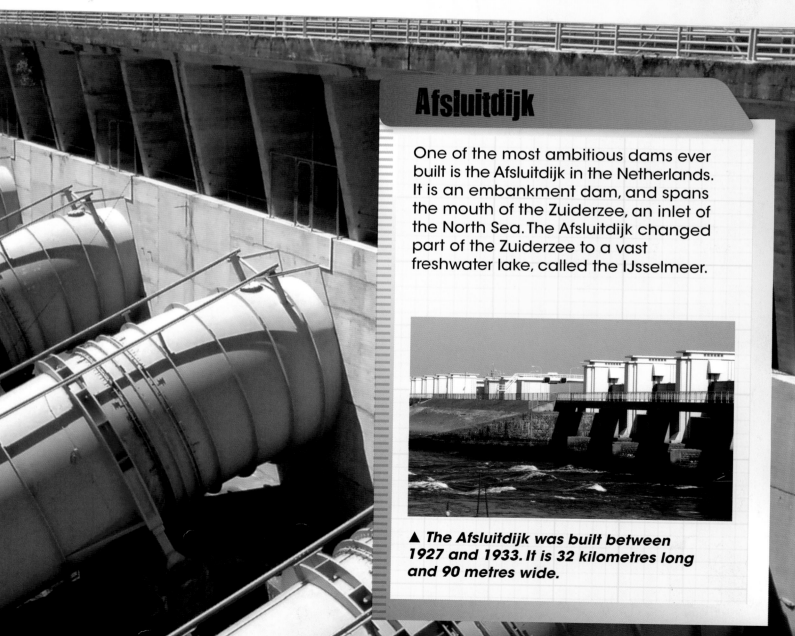

Afsluitdijk

One of the most ambitious dams ever built is the Afsluitdijk in the Netherlands. It is an embankment dam, and spans the mouth of the Zuiderzee, an inlet of the North Sea. The Afsluitdijk changed part of the Zuiderzee to a vast freshwater lake, called the IJsselmeer.

▲ The Afsluitdijk was built between 1927 and 1933. It is 32 kilometres long and 90 metres wide.

Dams

Dams are massive structures built across rivers and other bodies of water. There are three main types of dam: arch dams, embankment dams and gravity dams. The choice of dam depends on the amount of water to be held back, the shape and type of the surrounding ground and the cost of construction.

Arch dams

An arch dam is a curved wall made of reinforced concrete. It is a bit like an arched bridge lying on its side. The great weight of water pressing against the wall tries to push the ends of the wall outwards. The ends must be firmly anchored in position so that they cannot move. The ideal place for an arch dam is a narrow **canyon** with steep walls of rock on each side. An arch dam can have just one arch, or it can be built from a series of arches. The Daniel-Johnson Dam in Quebec, Canada, is an arch dam with 13 arches.

Gravity dams

A gravity dam stays in place because of its weight and shape. Gravity dams are made from concrete or stone. They can be built in the shape of arch dams and this type of dam is called an arch-gravity dam. The Hoover Dam in the USA is an example of an arch-gravity dam.

Embankment dams

Embankment dams rely on their weight to resist the force of water pushing against them. Embankment dams are made of **compacted** earth. To stop water seeping through, there is a layer of waterproof material on top of the dam or inside it. The waterproof material might be concrete, steel or plastic.

▼ To produce electricity, water from the reservoir behind a dam is channelled through pipes, called penstocks, to a turbine. The force of the water spins the turbine.

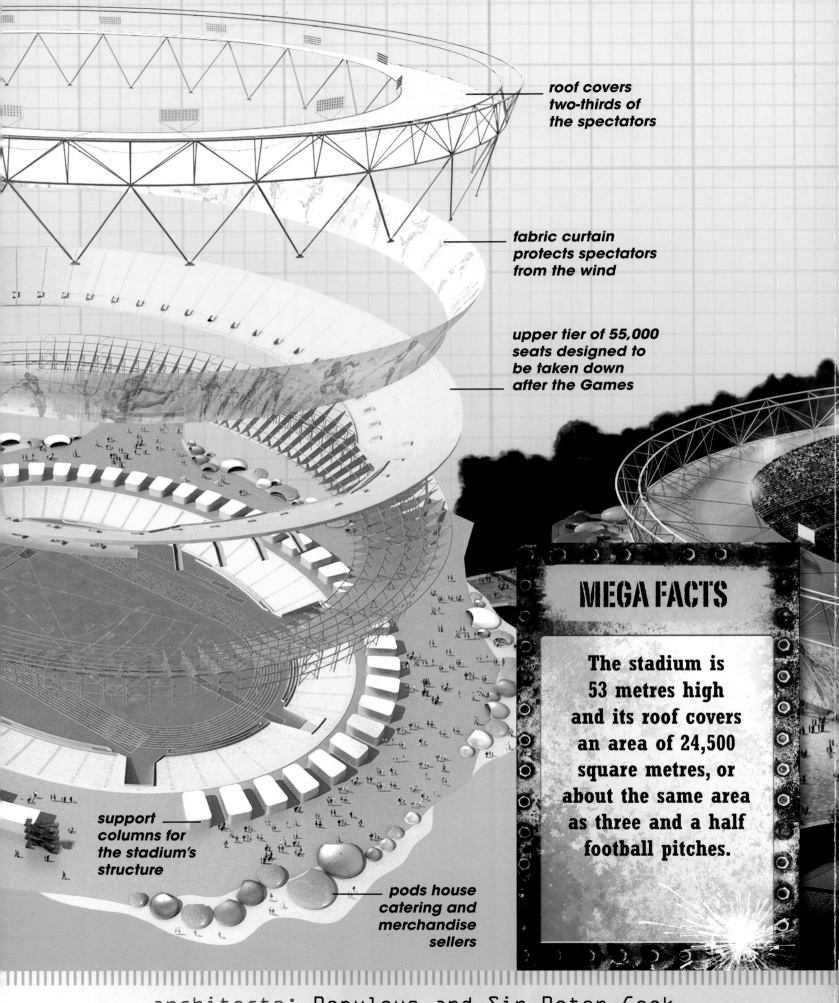

roof covers
two-thirds of
the spectators

fabric curtain
protects spectators
from the wind

upper tier of 55,000
seats designed to
be taken down
after the Games

support
columns for
the stadium's
structure

pods house
catering and
merchandise
sellers

MEGA FACTS

The stadium is
53 metres high
and its roof covers
an area of 24,500
square metres, or
about the same area
as three and a half
football pitches.

architects: Populous and Sir Peter Cook

Powerhouse

The last part of the dam to be built was the **powerhouse**, where electricity would be generated. The tunnels were blocked, so the Colorado River followed its natural course again. A new lake called Lake Mead filled up behind the dam. When the water was deep enough, it entered four tall intake towers and flowed through the turbines. The spinning turbines powered the electricity generators.

▲ *A row of huge turbines spin in the powerhouse.*

location: Black Canyon, Colorado River, USA

Mega workplaces

The biggest buildings on Earth are not cathedrals, monuments or sports stadiums. They are workplaces, such as factories and office buildings. The world's largest planes are built in massive buildings. The Pentagon, a US government office building, is the world's biggest office building.

Building spacecraft

The Vehicle Assembly Building (VAB) in Florida, USA, is the world's largest single-storey building, at 160 metres high, 218 metres long and 158 metres wide. It was built at the Kennedy Space Center in the 1960s to assemble the Saturn V rocket, which was used to launch the Apollo space missions. Its giant overhead cranes can lift rockets and spacecraft weighing up to 227 tonnes.

◄ The Kennedy Space Center's VAB has the world's biggest doors. Each of the four doors is 139 metres high.

Mega factory

Boeing's airliner factory in Everett, Washington State, USA, is the largest building in the world by volume (the amount of space inside it). It is more than twice the size of the next biggest – the factory in France that builds the world's biggest airliner, the Airbus A380. The Everett plant covers 13.3 million cubic metres – the whole of Disneyland could fit inside with room to spare.

▲ *Thirty thousand people work at Boeing's Everett assembly plant, the biggest factory in the world.*

The Pentagon

The Pentagon, headquarters of the US Department of Defense, is the world's biggest office building by floor area (604,000 square metres). About 23,000 people work in the Pentagon, so named because of its five-sided shape. It has five floors above ground level and another two below ground. It was built during World War II (1939–45). Steel was in short supply then, so the Pentagon's concrete structure was reinforced with as little steel as possible.

▲ *Because of its shape, it takes no more than seven minutes to walk between any two offices in the Pentagon.*

MEGA FACTS

The Kennedy Space Center's Vehicle Assembly Building is designed to withstand hurricane-force winds. It stands on 4225 steel piles.

Artificial islands

People started making artificial islands in the Stone Age, thousands of years ago. Small islands were constructed by piling up rock and earth in shallow water. Compared to the hand-built islands of past times, today's artificial islands are monsters. They are built to provide new land for homes, hotels and airports.

▼ *The artificial Palm Islands in Dubai, UAE, are made of sand. A circular breakwater, made of rock, protects them from the waves.*

Polders

The Dutch are the masters of reclaiming land from the sea and lakes. The area to be reclaimed is enclosed by building an embankment called a dyke. Then the water is pumped out to leave dry land. Land reclaimed like this is called a polder. The Dutch have created more than 3000 polders in the past 1000 years.

The new land created by polders is very flat. With no hills to break the wind, they are ideal for windmills.

Palm Islands

Three artificial islands have been built off the coast of Dubai. They are the Palm Jumeirah, the Palm Jebel Ali and the Palm Deira. They are called the Palm Islands because they are shaped like palm trees.

▼ A dredger sprays sand to create one of the artificial islands that form the World. The water depth is up to 17 metres and each island stands 3 metres above sea level.

MEGA FACTS

The world's biggest artificial island is Flevopolder in the Netherlands. It covers an area of 970 square kilometres.

The World

The Palm Islands are not the only artificial islands off the Dubai coast. The World is a cluster of islands made in the shape of a map of the world. The whole 'map' measures 6 kilometres by 9 kilometres. Hotels and homes are being built on the islands.

Failures and accidents

The world's biggest structures are usually very safe, yet occasionally things go wrong. Dams and stadiums are massive structures, but the forces of nature are strong enough to find weak points in their materials or design, sometimes with disastrous effects.

◄ When the wind tore a hole in the roof of the BC Place Stadium in Vancouver, Canada, a worker likened the sound to 'elephants running through your living room'.

Buckling steel

The concrete and steel structure of a sports stadium has lighting, video screens, television cameras, loudspeakers and all sorts of other equipment attached to it. In 1995, while the Centennial Olympic Stadium in Atlanta, Georgia, USA, was being built, the steel beams holding up a huge tower of lights collapsed, killing a construction worker.

Flood damage

In 2009, heavy rains caused an unusually high build-up of water behind the Situ Gintung Dam in Indonesia. The dam gave way, and a wall of water rushed down the valley below. Dozens of people died in the flood.

The low-lying coastal city of New Orleans in the USA is protected from flooding by earth banks called **levees**. When Hurricane Katrina struck the city in 2005, its levees and flood walls failed in more than 50 places, letting huge amounts of water into the city. Nearly 1500 people died.

The roof

A stadium's roof can be its weakest point. In 2009, a year after the new Sultan Mizan Zainal Abidin Stadium in Malaysia was completed, part of the roof collapsed. The sound it made was so loud that stadium workers thought a plane from a nearby airport had crashed.

▲ After the levees broken by Hurricane Katrina had been rebuilt, water had to be pumped out of the flooded parts of New Orleans.

▲ The roof of the Sultan Mizan Stadium collapsed onto the spectator stand when its steel supports buckled and folded.

Future monsters

International sports events such as the Olympic Games and the football World Cup are held in a different city each time. Fantastic new sports stadiums are built for each event.

The huge cost of building and operating new stadiums means that designers have to make the best use of the land. In the past, stadiums lay empty between sports events. Today's stadiums are built along with shops, offices, hotels, restaurants and homes, so that they are busy all the time.

◄ The new stadium for French football team Olympique Lyonnais has been designed to have a large, glowing roof that changes colour.

Multi-purpose stadiums

Many stadiums built today are usually designed for one sport only – such as football, baseball or athletics. Future stadiums will be able to change their playing surface more easily so that different sports can be played. The lowest layer of seats might be able to slide back to reveal a running track. A grass football field can be built in sections and these might be slid outside to reveal a hard surface for pop concerts or even motor sports.

▼ *The 40,000-seater Olympic Stadium in Sochi, Russia, will host the opening and closing ceremonies of the 2014 Winter Olympics. Football matches will be held there during the 2018 World Cup.*

The 'IT' factor

▲ *At major tennis events such as Wimbledon large screens show computer-generated replays.*

Future stadiums will be wired for information technology (IT). Spectators will be able to watch the action on screens all over the stadium. They will also be able to download information and video clips to mobile telephones.

DARKEST DEPTHS
AND OTHER
UNDERGROUND
MEGASTRUCTURES

10 of the world's deepest digs and bores

Type of dig/bore	Name	Location/Depth
Deepest borehole	Kola Superdeep Borehole	Russia/12,262 m
Deepest oil well	Tiber oil well	Gulf of Mexico/10,683 m
Deepest mine	TauTona gold mine	South Africa/3900 m
Deepest European metal mine	Pyhäsalmi mine	Finland/1440 m
Deepest open-cast mine	Bingham Canyon mine	USA/1200 m
Deepest diamond mine	Wesselton mine	South Africa/995 m
Deepest undersea tunnel	Eiksund Tunnel	Norway/287 m
Deepest rail tunnel	Seikan Tunnel	Japan/240 m
Deepest hand-dug hole	The Big Hole diamond mine	South Africa/215 m
Deepest subway tunnel	Pyongyang Metro	North Korea/110 m

Digging down

Deep holes are dug in the ground to get at fossil fuels such as coal and oil. Deep tunnels may be excavated to safely dispose of dangerous materials such as the **radioactive** waste from nuclear power stations. Tunnels also allow cars or trains to travel underneath mountains or seas.

Mining

Mines are dug to bring valuable and useful materials up from deep underground. Most of these materials are part of the rock itself. Rock is made of **minerals**, and some minerals contain the metals and other substances that we want to use. These minerals are called ores. Mines are dug down to reach the rock that contains the valuable ores.

MEGA FACTS

As long as 2000 years ago, the Chinese drilled holes in the ground to reach water. They used bamboo drill pipes fitted with iron cutting bits at the end.

Drilling

Coal and minerals have to be cut out of the ground, but oil and gas will come to the surface by themselves. If a hole is drilled down to oil and gas trapped underground, the pressure will squirt them all the way up to the surface. Scientists drill holes in the ground to bring up samples of earth, rock and ice for research. Water pumped down drill-holes can be heated by hot rocks deep underground. When the hot water comes back up to the surface, the heat can be used to warm buildings or to make electricity.

▲ Oil workers connect a pipe to the drill in order to collect oil that is forced to the surface from deep underground.

Tunnelling

Deep tunnels allow cars and trains to pass underneath mountains, rivers and even the sea. Deep tunnels are also used to store dangerous substances. Nuclear reactors produce waste that cannot be thrown away like ordinary rubbish because it is radioactive. This means that it gives out dangerous rays and particles. One way to deal with it is to store it in deep tunnels. The Waste Isolation Pilot Plant in New Mexico, USA, stores radioactive waste in underground tunnels 650 metres below the surface.

▲ *Drums full of radioactive waste arrive at the bottom of a shaft 650 metres underground in the Waste Isolation Pilot Plant in New Mexico.*

▼*The tunnels in mines are big enough for mechanical diggers, drilling machines and even trains to fit inside.*

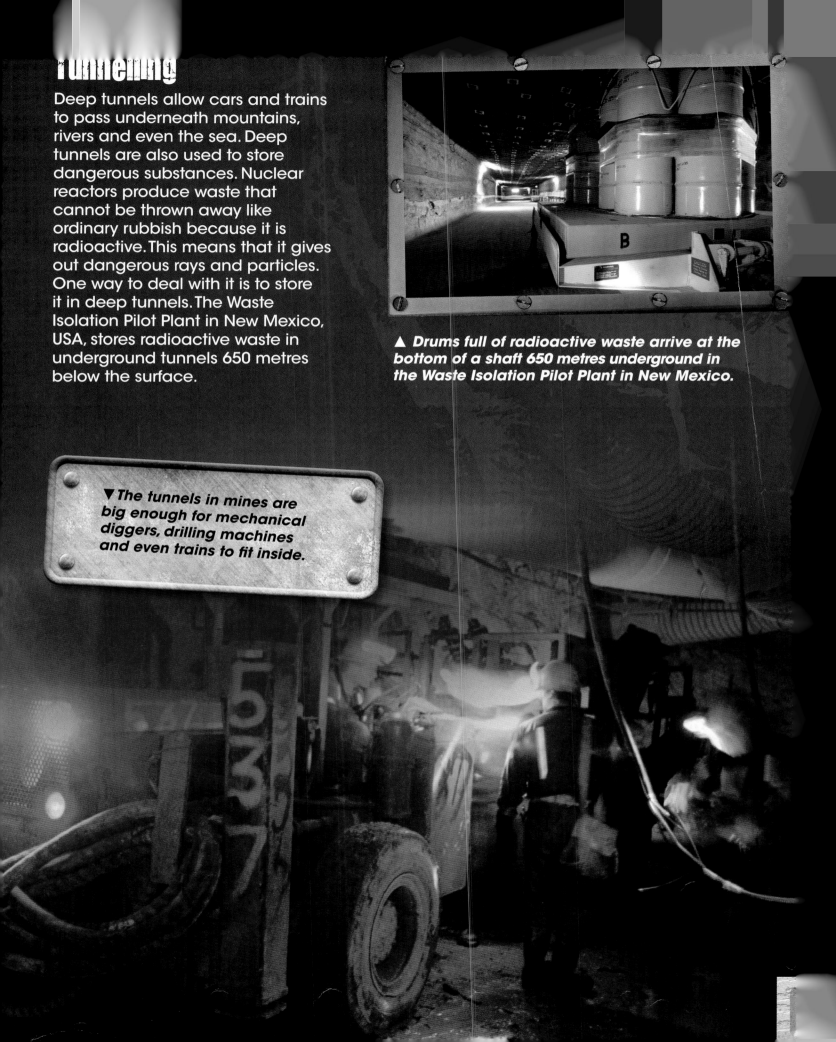

Deep challenges

The immense pressure deep underground creates a lot of difficulties for deep digging or drilling. Rock can fly out of a mine's walls, oil and gas can erupt from a well like lava from a volcano, and tunnels can cave in as they are being dug.

▼ In April 2010, an underwater blow-out caused the Deepwater Horizon oil rig in the Gulf of Mexico to explode.

Rock burst

Rock at great depths underground is squashed by the weight of all the ground above it. When a deep mine is dug, the huge weight pressing down on it can make rock explode out of its walls. Called **rock burst**, it is a great danger in the world's deepest mines.

◄ In deep mines, rock that looks dangerous, perhaps because it is cracked, can be covered with steel mesh or blown out with explosives before it bursts.

Blow-outs

Oil and gas trapped deep underground are under tremendous pressure. When an **oil well** is drilled, the oil or gas cannot be allowed to gush out of the top of the well. A safety valve called a **blow-out** preventer is fitted to the top of a well. If oil or gas tries to gush out – an emergency called a blow-out – the blow-out preventer seals the well.

Cave-ins

Tunnelling near rivers or the sea is dangerous because the soft ground can cave in. In the 19th century, the **tunnelling shield** was invented to solve this problem. The shield was an iron frame as big as the tunnel, and it held up the walls and roof while the tunnellers dug. Then the whole frame was pushed forwards, the newly dug part of the tunnel was lined with bricks, and tunnelling continued. Modern tunnelling machines still have a shield to prevent the tunnels from caving in.

▶ *The tunnelling shield held up a tunnel's roof while the men inside it dug the tunnel.*

MEGA FACTS

In 2008 an underground railway tunnel being dug in China collapsed, and a hole 75 metres across opened up in the road above it.

Tunnelling deep

Digging a deep tunnel involves cutting through solid rock. Until the 1960s, tunnels were dug by using hand-held drills, explosives, picks and shovels. It was a long, slow process and very hard work. Today, most long, deep tunnels are built by tunnel boring machines (TBMs).

▼ TBMs can tunnel through soft and hard rock, but if the rock is too hard, explosives are used instead.

Boring machines

The TBMs used today are as big as the tunnels they make. The front of the machine is a disc called the cutter head, which is covered with rows of teeth made of a very tough metal called tungsten carbide. The cutter head rotates slowly, about once every 10–15 seconds, and the teeth cut through the rock. The rock, now called spoil, falls onto a conveyor belt inside the TBM. The moving belt carries the spoil to the back of the machine, where a train takes it away to the surface. Meanwhile, the TBM moves forward and pushes the rotating cutter head against the rock.

Lining

Whichever construction method is used, the tunnel is then lined. In the past, tunnels were lined with bricks. Today, they are usually lined with concrete blocks. The blocks are bigger and stronger than bricks, and also faster to put in place.

MEGA FACTS

The biggest TBMs are almost 16 metres in diameter. With all the back-up systems that trail behind them, they can be 250 metres long.

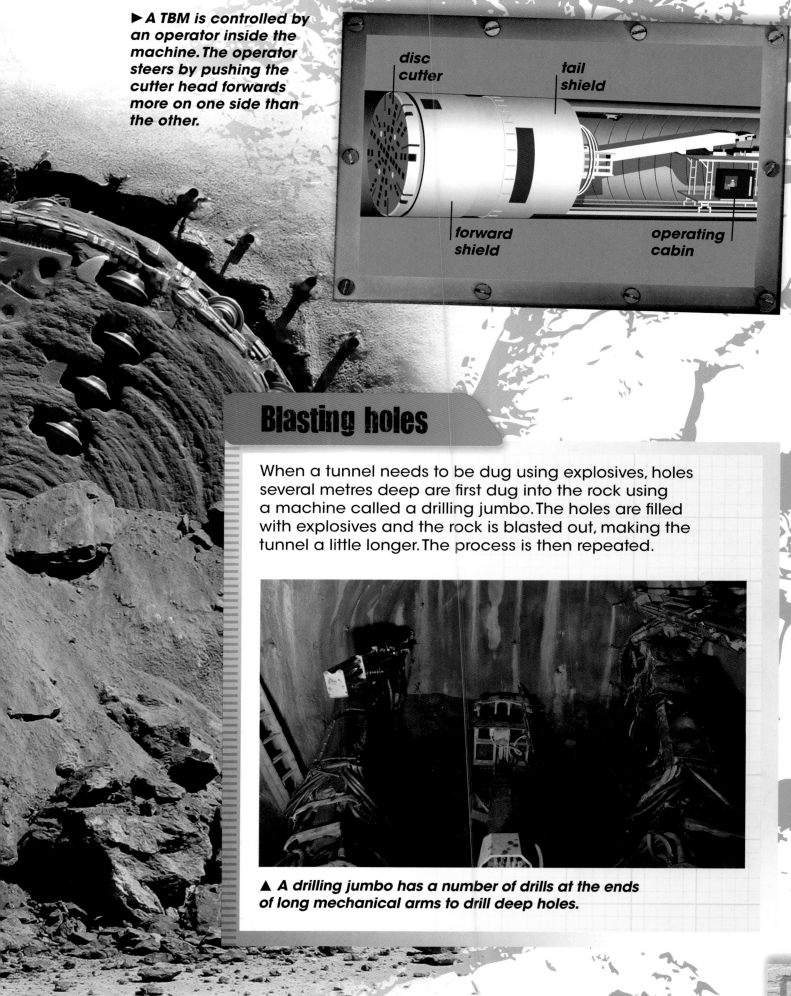

► *A TBM is controlled by an operator inside the machine. The operator steers by pushing the cutter head forwards more on one side than the other.*

disc cutter

tail shield

forward shield

operating cabin

Blasting holes

When a tunnel needs to be dug using explosives, holes several metres deep are first dug into the rock using a machine called a drilling jumbo. The holes are filled with explosives and the rock is blasted out, making the tunnel a little longer. The process is then repeated.

▲ *A drilling jumbo has a number of drills at the ends of long mechanical arms to drill deep holes.*

Mining for minerals

The surface of the Earth is made of rock, which contains minerals made of useful materials such as metals. Minerals and other materials, such as coal, are cut from the ground by mining. If minerals are near the surface, they can be reached by removing the earth above them. This is called open-cast mining. If they are deeper underground, shafts are dug down to them and tunnels dug out sideways from the shafts.

◄ A miner places explosives in holes drilled into the wall of a zinc and silver mine.

▲ A longwall shearer moves back and forth along a coalface cutting out the coal.

Mining methods

When miners started digging deep mines, they had to find a way to stop the roof falling in on them. One of the methods they used is called room and pillar. Chambers called rooms were dug out, leaving pillars of rock between them to hold up the roof. The room-and-pillar method is still used in salt mines today.

Coal is mined using a method called longwall mining. A line of props up to 400 metres long, called powered roof supports, holds up the roof. A machine called a shearer moves along the line of roof supports with whirling cutters, tearing out the coal. The coal falls onto a conveyor belt, which carries it away. While the shearer cuts the coal, other machines dig the mine's tunnels.

Mining rare minerals

The longwall mining method cannot be used to mine rare minerals and metals such as gold. There is not enough gold in one place to make it worthwhile using the huge machines used in coal mining, and the rock in gold mines is also too hard for them. Instead, the rock is shattered by explosives.

▲ *Miners use hand-held drills to dig into the rock face in the Western Deep gold mine in South Africa, which is 2500 metres deep.*

MEGA FACTS

During your lifetime, you will use about 14,800 kilograms of iron, 12,800 kilograms of salt and 360 kilograms of lead – most of which is dug out from mines.

Working underground

Mining is one of the world's most dangerous jobs. The hazards miners face deep underground include fires, explosions and cave-ins. Big, powerful machines are used in small spaces close to workers, the tunnels and shafts are difficult to escape from in an emergency, and dangerous gases can build up inside a mine.

Collapse in Chile

On 5 August 2010, part of the San José mine in Chile collapsed. For 17 days, nobody knew if the miners were dead or alive. Then a probe lowered down a hole came back up with a note attached.

It said that all 33 miners were alive, but they were trapped 622 metres below the surface. A shaft was drilled down to them and a specially built rescue capsule, called Phoenix, was lowered down the shaft to bring up the miners, one by one. By the time they were rescued, they had been trapped underground for more than two months.

◄ Miners trapped in the San José mine were rescued using the Phoenix. The capsule was big enough for just one person to get inside.

Fire and explosion

When the ground is disturbed by digging, gases are released. These include flammable gases such as methane, which can catch fire or explode. Mines have to be **ventilated**, using special ventilation tunnels, to stop these gases building up to dangerous levels.

▲ *Coal miners in Pakistan use wooden beams to secure the roof of the mine.*

Heat and air

The deeper you dig into the ground, the hotter it is. The rising temperature as you go deeper underground is called the **geothermal gradient.** Because of the geothermal gradient, the deepest mines are very hot. At a depth of 3660 metres, the walls of a mine can be as hot as 65 degrees Celsius. Miners are able to work only if cool air is blown through the mine.

▲ *In an emergency, miners trapped underground can be pushed to safety through ventilation tunnels.*

MEGA FACTS

The centre of the Earth, 6400 kilometres below your feet, is 6000 degrees Celsius, which is as hot as the surface of the Sun.

The Bingham Canyon Mine is an open-cast mine near Salt Lake City in Utah, USA. More than a kilometre deep already, and getting deeper by the day, it is the world's deepest open-cast mine.

The rock that is mined at the Bingham Canyon Mine contains copper ore, which is a mineral from which the metal copper can be extracted. The rock also contains smaller amounts of silver, gold and platinum. Surrounding the mine are grinding mills, a smelter and a refinery, where the metals are extracted from the rock and ores.

MEGA FACTS

The holes for the explosives in the Bingham Canyon Mine are drilled in very precise locations by machines guided by satellites in space.

Bingham Canyon Mine

width: 4 kilometres   depth: 1.2 kilometres

Undersea tunnels

Tunnels can be built to let cars and trains travel under the sea. They are dug through the rock beneath the seabed. The deepest undersea tunnels are the Seikan Tunnel in Japan and the Eiksund Tunnel in Norway.

The Seikan Tunnel

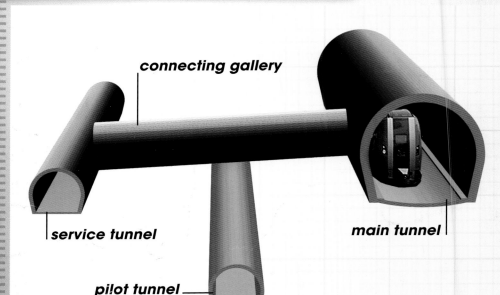

connecting gallery

service tunnel

pilot tunnel

main tunnel

◄ The main tunnel is horseshoe-shaped for most of the route, but it is circular in areas with difficult rock formations as this is a stronger shape.

By the 1960s, the number of people crossing the Tsugaru Strait between the Japanese islands of Honshu and Hokkaido was growing fast. More than 4 million people were crossing by ferry every single year. It was decided to build a tunnel. Construction of the Seikan Tunnel began in 1971. A small **pilot tunnel** was dug first, then a **service tunnel** and finally the rail tunnel through which trains would travel. Two stations were built inside the tunnel. They were the first railway stations ever built under the sea. The Seikan Tunnel opened in 1988.

MEGA FACTS

The Seikan Tunnel is 53.85 kilometres long. Some 23.3 kilometres of this is below the seabed. In places, the tunnel lies 140 metres under the seabed.

The Channel Tunnel runs beneath the English Channel between the UK and France. Construction work began in 1987. The Channel Tunnel is actually three tunnels – two 7.6-metre-wide railway tunnels, with a 4.8-metre service tunnel between them. The service tunnel provides access for workers and serves as an escape route in an emergency. The rail tunnels are linked to each other every 250 metres by small tunnels, called piston relief ducts. These let air being pushed along in front of a train escape into the other tunnel.

MEGA FACTS

Every day, 2.5 million readings are taken from 500 sensors inside the Channel Tunnel to make sure that there is no build-up of dangerous gases.

▼ *Specially designed trains run through the Channel Tunnel at up to 160 kilometres per hour.*

The Channel Tunnel

total length: 50 kilometres

Britain

chalk marl

English
Channel

France ___

Tunnel

▲ **The Channel Tunnel follows a layer of rock called chalk marl. The tunnel boring machines (TBMs) were steered left, right, up and down to stay within this layer.**

Planning the route

To plan exactly where and how deep the tunnel would have to go, geologists needed to know what types of rock were under the seabed and how deep and how thick these layers were. They found this out by setting off small explosions and watching how the sound bounced off the various layers of rock.

◄ **A 450-tonne TBM is lowered down a shaft at Sangatte in France to begin work on the tunnel.**

Rock to metal

The mine is worked all year round. First, the ground is shattered by explosives. The rock blown out by the explosives is crushed to a fine powder. The powder is added to tanks of water, where the metal particles float on top and the worthless rock particles, called **gangue**, sink to the bottom. The metal-rich water, called slurry, is sent along a pipe to a smelter. This is a type of furnace where the different ores are melted and separated. The metals are then separated from the ores at the refinery.

▼ *Blasting creates lines of terraces called benches. The benches higher up are set back to stop the walls from collapsing.*

Transporting blast rock

The rock blown out by the explosives is scooped up by mechanical shovels and loaded into giant trucks, which carry it away to be processed. Every day, 408,000 tonnes of rock are removed. The trucks take the rock to a crusher.

▲ *A steady stream of trucks carries rock to the crusher and then returns for more. The biggest of these trucks can carry 290 tonnes of rock.*

rn
el

ce
el

ss-
ge

◀ The lights of a train as it approaches the Tappi-Kaitei station in the Seikan Tunnel. The station sits on the Honshu side of the Tsugaru Strait.

▲ The Eiksund Tunnel also transports heated water and steam from the Amager Power Station under the sea to the Danish capital city of Copenhagen.

nnel for trains, but the Eiksund
nnel under the Vartdals Fjord
e Norwegian mainland. The
of 287 metres below sea level.
nnel was made using
of rock were blasted out. There
0 tonnes of explosives. The
ce by driving long bolts into the
er of concrete. Construction of
ginning of 2007. A three-lane
ened to the public in 2008.

Crossovers

Once the tunnels had been bored, two giant underground caverns called crossovers were created. If there is a problem in one tunnel, only part of the tunnel has to be closed. Trains can run in the rest of the two tunnels, using the crossovers to switch tracks and get round the trouble-spot. Each crossover is taller than three double-decker buses stacked on top of each other.

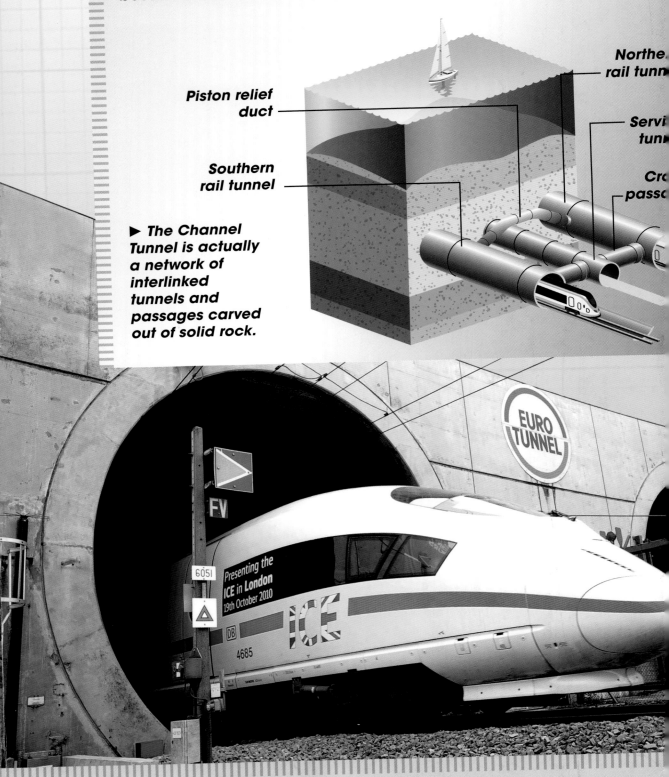

Northe..
rail tunn..

Piston relief
duct

Servi..
tun..

Southern
rail tunnel

Cro..
pass..

▶ **The Channel Tunnel is actually a network of interlinked tunnels and passages carved out of solid rock.**

EURO
TUNNEL

FV

6051

Presenting the
ICE in **London**
19th October 2010

ICE

DB

4685

Boring from each end

Tunnelling was carried out by 11 giant TBMs. Six of them bored the undersea part of the tunnels – three started from each end and headed for the middle. Up to 2400 tonnes of rock was brought out of each end of the tunnel every hour. On the French side, it was mixed with water to form slurry, which was piped across the countryside and poured into a lagoon. On the British side, it was piled up on the shore, where it formed a new piece of land. The machines boring the rail tunnels met in May and June 1991.

▲ When finished, the Channel Tunnel was 50 kilometres long.

▲ The curved lining segments were hoisted into place against the tunnel wall. Cement was pumped behind the segments to fill any small gaps.

Famous digs

Some of the darkest depths dug or drilled into the Earth's surface are famous because of their history or their great depth. The most famous mines, tunnels and drilled holes include the TauTona Mine, the Holland Tunnel and the Kola Superdeep Borehole.

▲ Miners walk from one elevator shaft to another on their way to the bottom of the TauTona mine, the world's deepest.

Record-breaking mine

The TauTona gold mine in South Africa is the world's deepest mine. The lowest part of the mine is 3.9 kilometres underground. Miners working in the lowest level have to take an hour-long journey by lift to reach the surface. The temperature at the bottom of the mine can reach 55 degrees Celsius. Air conditioners take in this air and cool it to 28 degrees Celsius to make it possible for miners to work.

MEGA FACTS

The Holland Tunnel was fitted with 84 ventilation fans – 42 blow in fresh air and 42 suck out stale air. The air in the tunnel is replaced every 90 seconds.

▲ The Holland Tunnel, which opened in 1927, was the world's first underwater road tunnel. It is 2.6 kilometres long.

Going superdeep

In the 1970s, scientists in the Soviet Union drilled the deepest hole in the **Earth's crust**. The Kola Superdeep Borehole is 12,262 metres deep. Drilling was stopped in 1992 because the rock at the bottom was too hot. It was 180 degrees Celsius – nearly twice as hot as boiling water. Had they continued drilling down to the target of 15,000 metres, scientists calculated that the temperature would have reached 300 degrees Celsius!

▶ *A special commerative stamp was released in 1987 to celebrate the digging of the Kola Superdeep Borehole.*

The Holland Tunnel

In the early 1900s, ferries crossing the Hudson River between New York and New Jersey were carrying 30 million vehicles a year. It was clear that a permanent link was needed to carry this traffic, so the Holland Tunnel was built. Tests revealed that the carbon monoxide gas given off by car engines was lethal, so fresh air had to be pumped in to clear out the dangerous fumes. The tunnel opened in 1927 and is still in use today.

Drilling

The oil and natural gas that fuel the modern world formed deep underground. They are brought up to the surface by drilling holes in the ground. Scientists drill deep holes in the ground too, to learn more about the Earth and its past.

Oil and gas are found by looking for the right kind of rocks in the ground. Geologists search for two types of rock, called reservoir rocks and cap rocks. Reservoir rocks are porous, which means that they have holes in them. The oil and gas fill the holes, like a sponge full of water. The right sort of rock must also form above the oil and gas to stop them bubbling up to the surface. This cap rock traps the oil and gas underground. When oil and gas are found, a hole is drilled down to them by a metal pipe with a toothed drill bit at the end. The drill is held by a tower called a **derrick**. Once the drilling rig strikes oil or gas, the top of the well is fitted with a series of valves to control the flow of oil or gas.

MEGA FACTS

The deepest ice core was drilled in Antarctica in 1998. It is 3623 metres deep. The deepest ice in the core fell as snow about 420,000 years ago.

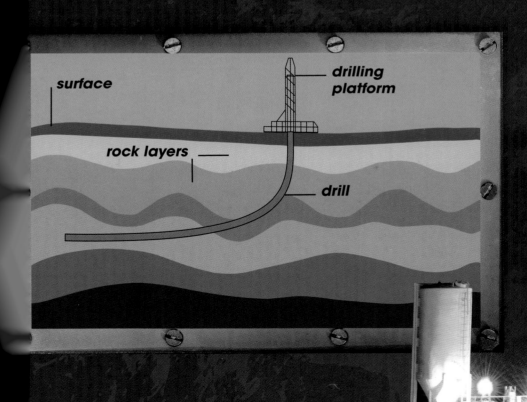

surface

drilling platform

rock layers

drill

◄ Drills do not have to go straight down. The end of a drill can be steered. This is called directional drilling. It is used where a drilling platform cannot be placed directly above an oil or gas field.

engine

Ice cores

Holes are drilled through ice with a hollow drill-pipe. When the drill is pulled up, the ice inside the pipe, called an **ice core**, comes up with it. The ice was once snow that fell on the ground. The weight of new snow on top squashed the snow underneath and changed it to solid ice. The deeper the ice, the older it is.

Scientists study ice cores to learn about the climate in the past. The thickness of the layers of ice in the core shows how much it snowed every year. Little bits of plants, particles of soot or ash and even bubbles of ancient air trapped in the ice give more clues.

▲ *These scientists are drilling an ice core on a mountain-top in Bolivia. The drill is powered by electricity made by solar panels.*

derrick

turntable

◄ *Inside the derrick, a turntable turns the pipe. The pipe turns a tough cutter called a drill bit.*

Thunder Horse is an **oil field** in the Gulf of Mexico. It was discovered in 1999 by a drillship called *Discoverer 534*, and is one of the deepest oil fields ever found.

Drillships search for oil by drilling holes called exploration wells. *Discoverer 534* lowered its drill to the seabed and drilled down 7850 metres before it struck oil. Another drillship, the *Discoverer Enterprise*, drilled a second exploration well and also struck oil. A production platform was brought in to extract the oil. The production platform is called the Thunder Horse PDQ (production drilling quarters). It is a giant structure in which up to 229 people can live and work.

Flame boom

Derrick

Crane

Towing tug

▲ *The Discoverer Enterprise drilled one of the first wells in the Thunder Horse oil field.*

Thunder Horse Oil Field

water depth: 1844.04 metres

Living
quarters

Lifeboats

Thunder Horse was due to begin producing oil and gas in 2005. However, the workers had to be taken off the rig because a hurricane was heading for it. When they returned, they found the platform leaning over at an angle. It was repaired quickly, but then cracks were found in pipes at the top of the well on the seabed. As a result, Thunder Horse began producing oil and gas only in 2008.

▲ *The Thunder Horse PDQ was tipped over in July 2005 by Hurricane Dennis.*

Supporting leg

▲ *The Thunder Horse PDQ is built on top of four massive legs that stand on a hull just under the surface of the water.*

MEGA FACTS

The Thunder Horse production platform produces enough oil to power the homes of 80,000 people.

Deep dangers

Deep mines and drill-holes can sometimes damage the land around them. Tunnels can cause problems for the vehicles that travel through them. Compared to the countless trillions of tonnes of rock and earth all around them, mines and drill-holes are tiny pinpricks in the Earth's crust. Even so, they can upset the delicate balance of underground forces.

Making quakes

Deep mines can change underground forces just enough to trigger an earthquake. A geothermal power plant in Basel, Switzerland, was closed down in 2009. It was believed to have triggered an earthquake under the city three years earlier. Coal mining may have triggered the biggest earthquake in Australia's history in Newcastle, New South Wales, in 1989.

▼ *In freezing cold weather, the heat inside a long, deep tunnel, such as the Channel Tunnel, can melt snow on a train.*

◄ *Work was stopped at the Deep Heat Mining geothermal experiment in Basel, after injections of high-pressure water triggered a small earthquake.*

The wrong kind of snow

Trains ground to a halt in the Channel Tunnel on 18 December 2009 due to cold temperatures outside the tunnel. Snow was blowing against the trains as they headed towards the French end of the tunnel. The power cars at the front and back of each train have ventilation grilles on each side to let in air for cooling. A sheet of material behind the grille normally stops snow getting through, but the snow on that night was so powdery that it got in. The warm air in the tunnel melted the snow, and the water ran into the electronic systems, which then broke down.

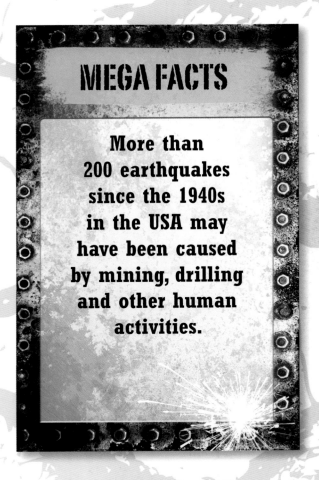

MEGA FACTS

More than 200 earthquakes since the 1940s in the USA may have been caused by mining, drilling and other human activities.

▲ *Digging deep holes in the ground, such as this old mine in Alaska, USA, is thought to trigger earthquakes, even in places where earthquakes are rare.*

Underground power

Holes drilled in the ground can be used to make electricity. The power stations that do this are called geothermal power stations. They make electricity using heat from deep underground, where volcanic activity can turn water into super-hot steam.

Drilling for heat

To use the heat, holes are drilled at least 3 kilometres deep into the ground. Cold water is pumped down some of the drill-holes. Deep underground, the water soaks up heat from hot rock. If the rock is hot enough, the water changes into steam. The hot water or steam comes back up to the surface through more drill-holes. The heat can be used to heat buildings or to make electricity.

MEGA FACTS

The first geothermal power station was built in Larderello, Italy, in 1904. Today, there are geothermal power stations in 24 countries.

▲ This geothermal power station in Iceland empties hot water into a nearby lagoon, where people bathe in waters that are at least 37 degrees Celsius all year round.

Power stations

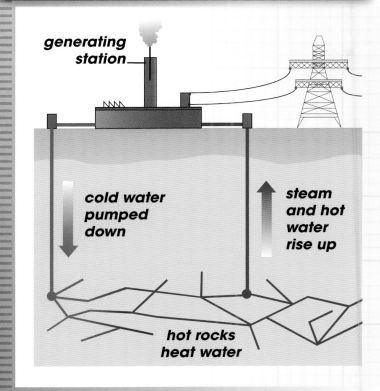

generating
station

cold water
pumped
down

steam
and hot
water
rise up

hot rocks
heat water

To make electricity, steam coming up out of the drill-holes makes drums, or wheels called turbines, spin very fast. The spinning turbines power generators, which make electricity. If there is not enough heat underground to make steam, the hot water is used to heat a different liquid that turns to a gas at a lower temperature than water.

◄ Geothermal power stations pump cold water into hot rocks deep underground.

The Geysers

The biggest group of geothermal power stations in the world is in California, USA, at a place called The Geysers. More than 350 wells have been drilled down to a depth of 3.2 kilometres. Water pumped underground comes back to the surface as steam for making electricity. After the steam has been used, it is not wasted.

The steam is cooled to change it back to water, which is sent underground again to make more steam and more electricity. The 22 geothermal power stations at The Geysers produce enough electricity for more than 1 million people.

Future digs

The undersea tunnels, deep mines and drill-holes that have been made in the Earth's crust are very ambitious projects, but there are even more amazing projects to come in the future. There are plans for undersea tunnels to join Japan and Korea, Europe and Africa, and the USA and Russia. Some future transport links, such as the new Hong Kong–Zhuhai–Macau link, will combine bridges with tunnels.

▶ *In the future, cars could drive through underwater tunnels held in place by tethers attached to floating pontoons.*

MEGA FACTS

The USA and Russia could be linked by a tunnel under the Bering Strait. Called the TKM-World Link, it would be about 100 kilometres long.

New tunnel projects

A tunnel could be built to link Japan and Korea. At 200 kilometres long, it would be the longest ever transport tunnel. The narrow sea channel between Spain and Morocco could be crossed by a tunnel. Linking Europe and Africa, the tunnel would be about 40 kilometres long and at least 300 metres below sea level. If it is built, it will be the world's deepest undersea tunnel.

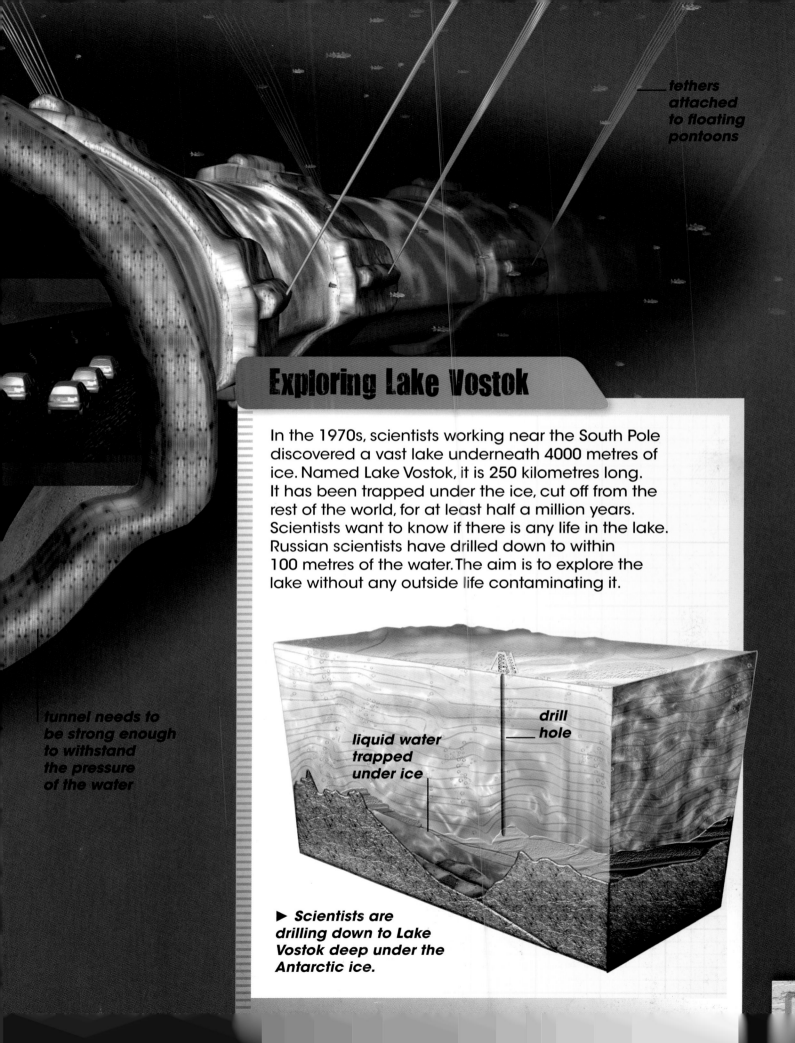

Exploring Lake Vostok

In the 1970s, scientists working near the South Pole
discovered a vast lake underneath 4000 metres of
ice. Named Lake Vostok, it is 250 kilometres long.
It has been trapped under the ice, cut off from the
rest of the world, for at least half a million years.
Scientists want to know if there is any life in the lake.
Russian scientists have drilled down to within
100 metres of the water. The aim is to explore the
lake without any outside life contaminating it.

tunnel needs to
be strong enough
to withstand
the pressure
of the water

drill
hole

liquid water
trapped
under ice

▶ Scientists are
drilling down to Lake
Vostok deep under the
Antarctic ice.

Glossary

abutment
A massive block of stone or concrete that holds an arch in place.

alloy
A mixture of a metal and one or more other elements. Steel is an alloy of iron and carbon.

amphitheatre
A building, which is usually circular or oval, in which tiers of seats rise from a central open arena.

anchorage
A massive concrete structure that holds a suspension bridge's cables firm.

antenna
The part of a radio that transmits or receives radio signals.

armature
A framework that holds up a sculpture or statue.

bascule
A type of drawbridge that opens upwards, with the weight of the bridge balanced by a large weight called a counterweight.

beam
A long, thick slab of wood, metal or concrete.

bedrock
Solid rock underneath the surface soil.

blow-out
An accidental, uncontrolled eruption of oil or gas from a well.

cantilever
A beam held up at one end only.

canyon
A long, narrow valley with steep sides.

cladding
A building's outer protective covering, usually not load-bearing.

compacted
Compressed or squashed together.

concourse
A wide hallway or corridor, or a large space where several pathways or corridors meet.

concrete
A construction material made of sand, gravel, cement and water. Reinforced concrete is strengthened by added steel mesh or wires.

curtain wall
A type of exterior wall used in the construction of skyscrapers. It hangs from the frame and does not bear any weight.

deck
The part of a bridge that people use to cross the bridge.

decking
Metal sheets that are covered with concrete to make a building's floors.

derrick
A tower on an oil or gas drilling rig, which is equipped with a crane or hoist for lifting sections of drill pipe into position.

dredge
To dig up gravel or silt from under water.

Earth's crust
The outermost layer of the Earth. It is 5–70 kilometres thick.

earthquake
Shaking and vibration of the Earth's surface caused by movement along a fault.

fjord
A long, narrow stretch of sea between steep valley sides, carved out by a glacier sliding down to the sea.

footprint
The area of the ground taken up by a building.

footway
The part of a road bridge that is used by pedestrians.

foundation
The lowest part of a structure. The foundations of a building bear the structure's weight and are normally below ground level.

gangue
Worthless unwanted rock mixed with a more valuable mineral.

gantry
A walkway or bridge-like structure, usually high off the ground, that links two building.

geologist
A scientist who studies rocks.

geothermal gradient
The rising temperature of the Earth at greater depths.

generator
A machine used to change motion into electricity.

girder
A strong beam, usually made of steel, used in the construction of bridges and other large structures.

grout
Thin mortar used to fill cracks and crevices.

guy
A wire or cable that anchors a radio mast to the ground.

hanger
A vertical cable or chain that links the deck of a suspension bridge to the suspension cables. Hangers are also called suspenders.

hazard
Any risk or danger; something that may cause damage.

hurricane
A tropical storm with winds that blow at more than 120 kilometres per hour.

hydroelectricity
Electricity that is produced using moving water to drive a turbine. The turbine powers a generator.

ice core
A cylinder of solid ice that is obtained by drilling down into ice.

levee
An embankment or wall built to hold back water.

load-bearing wall
Any wall that bears part of the weight of a building.

masonry
Any structure that is built from bricks, stone blocks or concrete blocks.

mineral
One of more than 4000 solid chemical substances that form rock.

oil field
An area where oil is found under the ground.

oil well
A hole drilled into the ground to bring up oil from an oil field.

pier
A support that holds up part of a bridge.

pile
A column buried in the ground to hold a building upright.

pilot tunnel
A small tunnel that is bored to test the ground where a tunnel is to be dug.

powerhouse
The part of a dam where electricity is generated.

radio mast
A tall structure, usually made of steel, with radio antennae at the top.

radioactive
Giving out radiation in the form of particles or rays as atoms change from one element to another element. This process is known as radioactive decay and it can be dangerous to humans.

reinforced concrete
Concrete that has steel mesh or wire embedded in it to make it a lot stronger.

reservoir
An artificial lake used for storing water. A reservoir can be created by building a dam across a river.

resonance
The tendency of an object to vibrate more and more violently at certain frequencies.

rivet
An iron or steel pin with a wide head at one end, used to fasten steel girders together.

roadway
The part of a road bridge that is used by vehicles, such as cars, buses and lorries.

rock burst
A sudden explosion of rock flying out of the wall of a very deep mine, caused by the enormous forces acting on the rock deep underground.

service tunnel
A tunnel that lets workers travel to any part of a road or rail tunnel.

solder
An alloy that is used to fuse (join) two metallic parts together.

stadium
A large structure where sports are played, with a playing surface surrounded by thousands of seats for spectators.

stay
One of the rods used to anchor a radio mast to the ground.

strait
A sea channel between two pieces of land.

substructure
The foundations of a tall building, which support it and hold it upright.

superstructure
The part of a tall building that is above the ground.

tier
One of two or more layers, one above the other. Tiered seating is rows of seats, one above another.

tower crane
A large crane, fixed to the ground on a concrete base, which is used to build tall structures.

tremor
A small earthquake.

tuned mass damper
A heavy weight that stops a building from swaying dangerously by moving in the opposite direction.

tunnel boring machine (TBM)
A giant vehicle with a rotating cutter head at the front that is used to dig a tunnel through the ground. A TBM is often custom-built to bore out a tunnel of a particular size.

tunnelling shield
A frame or structure that stops a tunnel's walls and roof collapsing while the tunnel is being dug.

turbine
A shaft or wheel with blades around the edge. When a liquid or gas flows through the blades, the turbine spins like a windmill in the breeze.

ventilation
Replacing stale air or fumes with fresh air.

viaduct
A bridge made from a line of arches or beams sitting on supports.

weld
To join metal or plastic parts together by melting the edges where they meet so that they run together and set as they cool.

Take it further

- Think about the materials used to build skyscrapers and towers. Why do you think these materials are used? Could other materials be used?

- If you were to design your own skyscraper, what shape would it be? Would it be an office block or full of homes? Would it be in a city or in the countryside? Why do you think there are no skyscrapers in the country?

- Is there a river near your home? What sort of bridge would you build across it?

- Why do you think most of the world's longest bridges are suspension bridges? Why are they not arch bridges or beam bridges?

- Think about why the longest bridges and tunnels are built. Would it be cheaper, easier and quicker to build a road over or around a mountain than to build a tunnel?

- Design your own sports stadium. What would it look like? How would you make it look different from other stadiums?

- Most scientists believe that air pollution caused by burning fossil fuels (coal, oil and gas) is changing the world's climate. Clean electricity produced by methods such as hydroelectric plants does not add to this problem. Find out which countries make the most hydroelectricity.

- Think about what the pyramids might have looked like if the Ancient Egyptians had been able to use modern materials such as concrete, steel, plastic and glass. Would they have been a different shape?

- If you could dig or drill a super-deep hole in the ground, where would it be and why would you dig it – to study rock deep underground, to search for gold, or another reason?

- Valuable minerals and oil have been found near the North Pole. Some people would like to drill wells and dig mines to reach them. Others think the risk of accidents are too great and these places should be left alone. What do you think?

Useful websites

www.skyscraper.org
The skyscraper museum has great pictures and information on the tallest buildings. Click on 'cool stuff for kids' for further information.

http://skyscraperpage.com/diagrams
Diagrams of the world's tallest buildings – including some not yet built.

www.longest-bridges.com
Log on to see pictures of and find out more about the world's longest bridges.

http://en.structurae.de/structures/stype
Links on bridges, viaducts, tunnels and more.

www.arizona-leisure.com/hoover-dam-building.html
Find out more about the building of the Hoover Dam.

www.london2012.com/webcams/
Watch the video clips to track the progess of the construction of stadiums for the London Olympics.

www.yourdiscovery.com/machines_and_engineering/tunneltrial/
Dig your own virtual tunnel with this interactive game.

http://encyclopedia.kids.net.au/page/mi/Mining
A great website all about mining.

Website information is correct at time of going to press. However, the publishers cannot accept liability for any information or links found on third-party websites.

Index